Praise for
Leaders in Motion
by M. C. Wilson

Wilson's vision of leadership inspires clarity and commitment. It is about reflection, action and drawing energy from the balance among all the forces pulling at you so that you can become world class leader. LEADERS IN MOTION is a guide for how to learn by living, how to lead by following and serving, and how to transform an organization by first transforming yourself. It is a must-read.
> —Rich Cober, Ph.D., Director
> Talent Management Analytics and Solutions
> Marriott International

In a business world immersed in technologic, economic and cultural change, LEADERS IN MOTION provides a roadmap for leveraging the increasingly diverse expertise needed to achieve great outcomes. M. C. Wilson's insights and advice for leaders come to life through real-world stories skillfully woven throughout the book.
> —Michael Gordon
> President, CC Pace

Leaving an imprint on the world around us is the kind of leadership all of us are called to achieve, whether at work or in our home communities. For that, I recommend LEADERS IN MOTION, a guide for discovering and cultivating the leader within—for the sake of releasing the unique contribution only you can make!
> —Reggie Gordon
> CEO, Greater Richmond Chapter of the
> American Red Cross

M. C. Wilson is one of the world's leading experts in organization leadership. She is an extraordinary example of the fact that integrity, courtesy and constant transformation are the key ingredients for unparalleled leadership and ongoing success. From her unassuming childhood through the many strong relationships she has with leaders across industries, Wilson draws important and valuable lessons from every story. Her book offers the reader a chance to benefit from this stellar leader's quiet, humble nature, which in turn will have tremendous impact on their success.

> —Stuart E. Greenberg, Ph.D.
> Global Pharmaceutical Market Research Director
> Multinational Diversified Healthcare Company

LEADERS IN MOTION provides a refreshing perspective, with a focus on integrity as the guiding principle for sustainable improvements in performance and results. Today's marketplace is global, competitive, technologically vibrant, and teeming with ideas and possibilities. Success depends on the ability of leaders to respond to opportunities without the constraints of ego or fear. Wilson's program provides leaders with an approach to align their objectives with these challenges, and includes a roadmap for how to win the race with good sportsmanship, civic responsibility and grace.

> —Roberta Keller
> Operational Excellence Advisor
> Customer Service Operation
> Dominion Power

To be a leader in any industry, corporations must have leaders at every level ready to focus on how to meet the evolving needs of valued customers. That challenge starts with working together in a way that fosters imaginative and quick-witted problem solving. As Wilson shows in LEADERS IN MOTION, imagination, wit, smart solutions and can-do energy start within each and every one of us, and have the greatest impact when we consciously choose to contribute and to lead.

> —Dennis Mabes
> Senior Vice President, Human Resources
> Danaher Motion Group

The primary benefit of reading LEADERS IN MOTION is the up close and personal chats the author has had with industry leaders who have cultivated cultures of transformation in their own work. In fact, throughout the book, Wilson's work in the trenches of organization design delivers time-tested wisdom from rock-solid leaders. This book is a must-read for anyone who wants to improve their own leadership abilities continuously.

> —Amy Means
> Director, Employment Development
> Lafarge

To ensure unrivaled productivity, those leading today's talented workforce must foster a dynamic work environment while providing personal balance and flexibility. That kind of leader always stands out among equals because they understand that the employee-employer relationship is a partnership. LEADERS IN MOTION is the perfect roadmap for mastering critical personal and interpersonal skills—all the way to sustainable success!

> —Maria Proestou
> CEO and President
> DELTA Resources

LEADERS IN MOTION is a book that teaches leaders—and those who seek to lead—how expressing authenticity and leading with intention can give us the courage and power to transform ourselves and our organizations. M. C. Wilson uses examples from her own life and those of famous leaders to show how we can effectively harness our energy, imagination and commitment to provide lasting victory over any challenge.

> —Roy Wood
> Retired Naval Officer and
> Former Defense Department Executive

Leaders in Motion

Winning the Race for Organizational Health, Wealth and Creative Power

By M. C. Wilson

Published by Transformation Systems, Inc., Arlington, Virginia
Printed in the United States of America.

Library of Congress Control Number: 2008911150

Wilson, M. C., 1963–

   Leaders in Motion: Winning the Race for Organizational Health, Wealth and
   Creative Power / M. C. Wilson

ISBN: 978-0-9821825-0-5

1. Business/Economics — 2. Leadership — 3. Motivational

Dedication

To my parents, Thomas and Jean Carter

Acknowledgments

Writing this book has been a creative evolution for me, and I've drawn on the energy and talent of many people who are leaders in their own spheres. I can mention only a few here.

I am constantly aware of my good fortune to work with many remarkable leaders as colleagues, mentors and clients. It is impossible to name everyone. To all our TSI clients, I offer my gratitude for your permitting me to serve your visions of transformation and for your contribution to the growing body of transformation science. I'm especially grateful to the leaders who have allowed me to interview them over the years, including those whose compelling stories and wisdom I've quoted in this book: Renny DiPentima, Hugh Gouldthorpe, Jr., Jim MacDonald, Paulette Maehara, Eileen McCaffrey, Liz Murphy, Bob Sledd, Dick Stieglitz, Bobby Ukrop, and David Wright.

Many colleagues in the industry have played defining roles in my commitment to supporting the success of transformational leaders. My colleagues at TSI are not only my partners in setting leaders in motion across the globe but also leaders themselves, who energize me and inspire me. In particular, I'm grateful to Trina Willard, Garry Coleman and Altyn Clark for their clarity, commitment and energy in the face of daily management and leadership challenges. I thank

Cindy Schilling for her unconditional friendship, constructive feed-back on this project, and ability to make every endeavor fun.

Special thanks to TSI's client organizations for providing the environment in which the transformation science body of knowl-edge can continuously develop.

I would also like to thank the professionals who have encouraged me to communicate my leadership philosophy in new ways, espe-cially Teresa Hartnett for her insight, patience and dedication. With-out her natural brilliance and gentle discipline, this book would not have been possible. Thanks, as well, to the people on her creative team: Martin Morse Wooster for his meticulous fact-checking, Judy Cleary for her thorough copyediting, and Catherine Campaigne for the graphic design.

And, closest to my heart, I thank my greatest inspiration, Bob Wilson, for his eternally positive nature and determination to make every thought, word and deed count.

Preface

As the founder of Transformation Systems, Inc., I serve as the leader among my valued colleagues, all of whom are experts in multidisciplinary transformation. We are regularly invited as catalysts to overhaul performance on individual, group and organizational levels. How do we do this? We do it by keeping leaders in motion.

Leaders in every area and at every level are facing a new world reality. They must match and beat the challenges of a globalizing economy by promoting a higher level of responsiveness to opportunities and challenges—and to constant change. To achieve ever greater resource efficiency in a high-paced technological age, they must inspire others intentionally and constantly to adapt as a way of life. Today, few organizations have extra time, money or other resources to invest in short-term changes. They want long-term change that will fuel itself. They want a culture of transformation.

TSI shows groups how the very culture around them can evolve into a state of continuous transformation. In this setting, the organization is vigilant, responding to contributions by its participants and to unexpected circumstances. Leaders stand out because they exercise the will to imagine what few dare to imagine. They imagine what lies beyond the possible. They are free to do so because they are prepared to rely on transformation that does not have an end.

TSI provides counsel and support for this kind of commitment to transformation. Our clients are organizations ranging from Fortune 500 corporations in all commercial industries to federal, state and local agencies, as well as a variety of nonprofits. Despite the diversity, these groups all share the same reality: Approaches that might have worked yesterday must adapt to a new and rapidly changing environment or they will become threats to current and future success. In our role as sounding board and co-visionaries, we help leaders recreate whole cultures for sustainable success, one decision at a time.

How we work is simple enough. Transformation is about decisions and actions and results. We work side by side with leaders—together, we are change agents. We challenge them to new awareness when they are making decisions, to new masteries when they are taking action, and to new daring when they imagine achievable results.

Our teams design and deliver customized solutions to problems. We make ourselves available to experience these problems in real time, on the premises with our clients. We integrate disciplines and functions so that every activity in the organization contributes to large-scale change right away and in the long term as well. Most important, in one-on-one coaching and in training groups, we challenge our clients to lead the way, living their transformation in their daily work life. In our work with groups of talented experts and dedicated staff, every contributor to transformation regularly steps into a leadership role, whether formal or informal. In our work, there are no followers.

Although the approach may be simple, the work is not easy, and transformation comes in many different forms. Some groups seek to move beyond plateaus and to grow. Others are growing rapidly and need to proceed on a more even keel. Still others must transform by cutting back and focusing on their core competency. And some are fighting to survive, facing the daunting challenge of getting performance back on track with no clear idea about next steps. Our clients want change to be more than an exercise in window dressing. They want transformation, and they usually want it right away. With willing clients, we can do a lot of good work as catalysts for transformation, and the impact of this work lasts long after we leave.

We rarely encounter a lack of willingness to change. Everyone is usually ready for it. And many people are ready to play short-term leadership roles to contribute to forward motion. They are anxious to rise to the occasion and lead discussions, task groups or informal interactions, and to make decisions. However, they may be hesitant because they're waiting for the right leader to emerge and chart a pathway to success. Often, they don't want to offend current leadership and are afraid that change means a change in the nameplate on the door to the executive suite. Fortunately, what is usually needed is for the current leaders—at every level—to tap into their full leadership potential.

We find that, initially, as groups are poised for change, they are also waiting. They may seem stalled, but they're just waiting for a leader to marshal their talents and create a setting that unleashes their expertise. They are ready to participate in transformation, and they want to contribute to the success of the undertaking, but they cannot do so without a leader. They're ready to assume their own informal leadership roles, but they're waiting for a leader.

Experience has shown us that the right solutions to organizational problems all start with leadership, usually with one stand-out leader—the person who is confident enough to propose an idea and inspire trust among all those who will participate in the transformation. This leader can empower an entire group of talented people to bring about change collectively. This is the person who makes the difference to higher management, too, because she is able to motivate every possible contributor to step out and make a difference every day. She encourages leadership all around her.

Leaders can be hard to find. Sometimes a person is transported into the organization from outside to lead. His new vision may energize the group or it may slow transformation irreparably. Sometimes a leader emerges as the organization moves toward change. What surprises our client organizations (and most executives) is how often leaders are already embedded in the organization unnoticed, underdeveloped and unaware of their own potential. They are waiting to be tapped. But regardless of where the leadership comes from, it is with leaders that transformation begins, and, as transformation catalysts, we begin our work with leaders.

The distance between any problem and its solution is short. Only a few basic steps are needed to start a transformation culture. The secret to successful transformation does not lie in complexity but in keeping leaders in motion. Leaders turn to me and my colleagues at TSI for assistance in creating positive change in their organizations. We point out that the world is in motion and that no one can lead forward toward success while standing still mentally, physically or spiritually. When a leader is in motion, he or she has made a conscious choice to make every thought, word and deed count. No part of any day is routine. This leader develops a personal discipline to stay alert, tapping every event for its full potential to expand awareness and to evolve consciously toward goals that are both personal and organizational. Once leaders are in motion, everyone around them is energized and motivated, and collective results and sustained achievement follow naturally.

At TSI, we specialize in keeping leaders in motion so they can lead organizations through change toward greater success. We partner with them to foster organizational cultures in which transformation is continuous and success is routine. Many of our clients have asked us to set down the basic elements behind our leadership coaching. I've written this book to help leaders at every level of every organization, large or small, kick off transformation for the long term by getting and staying in motion.

This book focuses on leaders, both formal and informal, who have the unique talent to empower everyone around them to participate as a full partner in transformation. Today's economy, with its insatiable need for great ideas and effective implementation, does not reward stifling environments and underdeveloped staffs. It demands smart work at full throttle. To unleash productive power, we look to leaders. Let the transformation begin.

Marta C. Wilson
Arlington, Virginia
January 2009

Contents

The Transformational Power of Leaders in Motion

Transformation has always been an ingredient of smart business practices. At TSI, we believe that in this century's new economic realities, transformation is not optional. It alone secures survival and advances growth.

Imagining has become mandatory. The economic environment in which organizations operate is globalizing very fast. Even local businesses must have an international mentality. To understand the world requires us to step beyond what we know and to welcome what we cannot imagine. Technology advances at a faster and faster pace. Life, work, and opportunities are improving exponentially, and at the same time growing more complicated. Every group must constantly practice technological vigilance, because the global working environment can be upended by one sudden shift into a previously unimagined technology. Indeed, imagining is mandatory.

The full potential of every resource must be mined for maximum benefit because, in such a highly competitive market, we cannot afford to let any potential go untapped. One of the greatest powers in the history of our nation's economy has been its creative force, its ability to imagine. The same is true of the future. Every person's full potential must be unleashed. Every function must be free to operate at full capacity and must be well aligned with group goals. Otherwise, an organization will waste its greatest resource—human creativity.

Creativity is mandatory. Leadership is not only an art; it also seeks to free the work of others to evolve toward creative heights.

In this setting, the deluge of information can be more confusing than meaningful. It is here where clarity, commitment and energy become crucial ingredients for any group endeavor. It is only with clarity, commitment and energy that potentially daunting challenges can become opportunities, not threats. How can we achieve clarity, commitment and energy? By creating a culture of transformation.

Transformation is leadership in motion. Initiating ongoing organizational transformation is about choosing to do whatever it takes to kick off momentum that achieves not just unimagined success in the near future but sustained success, year after year. It is about embedding transformation deeply within the group culture. How can we keep the momentum of transformation alive in an organization that seeks long-term success? By keeping leaders in motion.

If leaders keep moving, their power will be measured in group results. If leaders lack clarity, commitment or energy, their power will be measured in frustration, not success. Like a boulder in a fast-moving river, leaders can disrupt the flow, even divert the full force of energy into a destructive path—or they can be models of change for everyone. What people in the midst of transformation need to see is the inspiring model of leadership in motion.

Transformation is not a quick fix, although it can start out that way. It's a system of participation in which everyone is free to contribute all their best talent, knowledge, judgment and skill. It activates leadership qualities in every person. It reveals unrecognized leaders in the most unassuming workers. What it requires to start and continue is a singular type of leader, someone who can lead others as equals. This person is able to draw out the leadership potential of entire groups, so that everyone contributing to the momentum of change and improvement is free to do so without reservation. Everyone becomes part of a network of people in motion toward ever greater success. The sense of leadership and accomplishment are shared.

Exemplary leadership may be rare, but that's not because it is some kind of innate ability reserved to a very few people. Leadership can be learned, but people seldom embark on the quest to acquire leadership skills. Instead, if they seek advancement, they focus on acquiring more knowledge and subject matter expertise. Professionals who have mastered an area of expertise often rise to positions of authority. Their new job descriptions may assign them the role, but they are not necessarily authentic leaders—yet. However, at this point or any other point of in their careers, they can learn about being leaders and about the leadership qualities they already have. They can learn to challenge themselves to ever better leadership abilities and to practice new reactions to old circumstances with a heightened consciousness. They can play energizing roles in group dynamics so that the organization can move forward, not on their power alone but on the power of all.

Three types of mastery are required to lead an organization or an initiative. The first is mastery of the enterprise itself. *Enterprise mastery* is associated with having cutting-edge knowledge of all business functions, from accounting and marketing to products or services. It is about being a whiz at the nuts and bolts of running an organization, a division or a group. It is a requirement for the person who is officially in charge. Enterprise mastery is absolutely crucial, and it can be developed in the person who has advanced to a leadership position and is willing to learn. Whatever this person doesn't know on the first day of a new position can be outsourced. The real challenge is to be honest about needing help and self-confident enough to seek it. TSI works regularly with clients to expand enterprise mastery among their leaders and staffs. But we also remind clients about other leadership skills that can help take enterprise mastery to new levels.

The second type of mastery required to lead an organization is the one that everyone mentions most frequently: Leaders must have achieve *interpersonal mastery.* Leaders are seen as people who somehow affect the dynamic of a group to improve productivity and inspire spirit. The leader must be skilled at interactions with everyone from staff through executive management, from customers through colleagues and industry peers. At TSI, we agree that mastering interpersonal skills is crucial for organizational leadership, and we work with leaders and staff to develop them.

But we find in our group training and one-on-one coaching that interpersonal skills depend on the capacity of people to master themselves. At TSI, we preface leadership development and effectiveness training with a program in ***personal mastery.*** This is where we begin our work as catalysts for transformation.

To become an expert in one or more areas of an enterprise, a person must discipline herself to study and learn and excel. She will start by mastering herself. Before being able to interact effectively with others, she must develop some measure of self-modulation. This is the starting point, where a person has achieved a certain amount of enterprise mastery and interpersonal mastery. Now she is ready to focus on personal mastery, the crucial ingredient for leading a successful organization.

The most common complaints about new executives reflect a lack not of enterprise mastery but of something else. One complaint involves a manager with exquisite enterprise mastery who has been promoted to lead a group but has no interpersonal mastery and seems unable to evolve into the many roles of leadership. Another complaint involves a person who makes efforts to lead that seem inauthentic. He seems insincere, and his credibility suffers. It's as if the staff sees him wearing shoes 10 times too big for his feet. The only way to meet the challenge of being an authentic and effective leader is to be true to yourself first. The only way to fit into the new shoes is to evolve into the large role you've been given and grow with it as your success brings constant change.

The only way to do this is to master knowledge of yourself before you try to master the role of leader. You will find a leader within you, waiting to be discovered and developed from the inside out. This book offers insights into that evolutionary process and how it can unleash all the best talent in you and the people you're leading.

When you have developed a sense of clarity about yourself, you can inspire clarity in the people who depend on you for direction. You can project clarity to the networks of people involved in the group's endeavor. Only when you've tapped your own sense of commitment can you inspire the commitment and talent of others. When you have worked through obstacles within yourself, your energies will no longer be drained by your personal conflicts, and you will be able to enthusiastically channel the dynamism of staff, colleagues and groups toward positive ends. When you have achieved clarity, commitment and new energy, you are ready to lead, either in an official executive capacity or as an equal among many in a group. Whatever the setting, your clarity, commitment and energy will shine, and this is what a culture of transformation needs to flourish.

To transform a group, you must be on a transformation path yourself. Thus, personal mastery is the first step in organizational transformation. At TSI, we say that leaders who want to transform a group radically must be ready to be transformed radically themselves. Transformation is personal, and leaders who wish to succeed must radically personalize the transformation. To earn their place as leaders, they must begin by mastering themselves.

Throughout history, leaders have led people through tumultuous times in organizations and nations. President Abraham Lincoln and Prime Minister Winston Churchill are two prime examples. A study of their lives offers rich guidance for any leader who is seeking to transform an organization. Churchill and Lincoln both led during turmoil. The image of their seemingly unflappable courage in the midst of storm and uncertainty inspires us. Their disciplined efforts had historic impacts, and the clear decisions they made have created a legacy we can still appreciate today. Despite the confusion of events, they were able to choose and act with clarity, commitment and energy. These traits marked them as extraordinary leaders and enabled them to successfully deal with terrible challenges.

Other leaders can be the best teachers for those who seek to develop their leadership abilities. Every successful person I meet has at least one role model, even a hero. Mentors are invaluable to leaders. They can be found in our trek through education and industry, and drawn from our childhood experiences and our reading of history or biographies. No matter the source, we can tap into the qualities of other leaders to become better leaders ourselves.

This book is about transformational leadership, and it begins with a transformation that is up close and personal. It begins with personal mastery. We believe that personal mastery is the first step to interpersonal mastery and enterprise mastery—and to organizational achievement. Without personal mastery, leaders cannot be in motion and cannot stay in motion to make a difference. They must be willing to embark on a journey of personal mastery as a way of life if they are to inspire a culture of authentic transformation around them.

Mentors and role models appear in these pages in their own words. They inspire the path of personal transformation, which is the first step to authentic leadership.

When you dive deep into yourself to seek new levels of personal mastery, you begin to see how your own story becomes the focus of work—and the source of inspiration. So it seems only right that I begin this journey with you by sharing some watershed moments and some insights from my own story that have led me to my role as a leader of transformation catalysts.

Clients see me drive up in a new BMW, and colleagues perhaps make assessments about my standards and means. My biography includes degrees from prestigious academic institutions and an impressive client roster. The business I founded serves governments, nonprofits and corporations; employs brilliant people; and has its own publishing division. A typical day can involve traveling to two or even three cities for meetings or private consultations and an itinerary that can run from 4:00 AM to 9 PM. All this success is the direct result of in-depth and relentless transformation.

A watershed in my own transformation occurred in August 1994, when I founded (with guidance from two mentors, Scott Sink and Stephen Hacker) my corporation. There were no financial investors, and I had no key credit relationships. What I did have was my brain, my heart and my vision. That has proved to be enough for me, and it can be enough for any leader.

The years leading up to that day were very different. If anyone had seen the circumstances in which I lived when I was five years old, they would never have guessed that I'd run a multimillion-dollar organization. As I look back on myself, the daughter of humble and hard-working southern farmers, I understand why the philosophy of my organization includes a belief that leadership talent can lie hidden in the most unlikely candidate and can fuel the heroic survival of communities and organizations that have no outside support.

When I was six years old, my family moved from a farm into a town near Knoxville, Tennessee, with a shockingly large population of 40,000. My parents had been raised as farmers, but they believed that by moving to a town and finding jobs, they could give their children a better life and more opportunities. So they ventured to a place where the nature of daily life was radically different from the farms they had known and where they no longer had the rich social network of extended family and friends. They courageously sought transformation, despite the sacrifices involved.

The old phrase "no pain, no gain" comes to mind when I think of the discomfort the first steps of transformation can inflict on an organization. Every task can feel changed, and daily life can feel upended. It was like that for us kids, but much more so for our parents, who had left behind a way of life. My father went to work as a line foreman in a furniture factory, but he never considered his supervisory role as a way to distance himself from the hands-on work flowing through the production line. I remember him coming home at night with hands torn and bleeding from working with splintered wood. My father had clarity about many things. He did not believe he was above the men who worked for him. At one point, he joined his men in a picket line to obtain safer conditions, and he paid the same price they did when the strike failed—he lost his job. However, he won the esteem of his wife and children for standing up for a cause he believed was right and fair.

My father was also very clear in his determination to provide a better life for his family, and his commitment to us sustained him through hard times. Within a decade after moving, he had advanced financially and experientially to the point that, as I entered college, he was founding a catering business. It grew and flourished until he sold it to retire. His commitment to family made a deep and lasting impression on me about the value of personal sacrifice for the sake of others—and how it can improve our own lives in the process.

My mother never worked outside the home. Instead, she devoted her time and energy to caring for my twin brothers and me. I'm certain that much of my self-discipline comes from my mother, who was both role model and mentor. She believed in keeping one's commitments in the detail as well as the broad strokes, and she insisted on the importance of courtesy and etiquette in all human interactions. Every day, I use these and many other habits, attitudes and values that my mother instilled in me. Because I had such a mentor, I am committed to the process of mentoring. One of my roles now is to work with client organizations to cultivate authentic change and positive growth on every level by putting mentoring programs in place. There is no substitute for the experience of a win-win mentor-protégé relationship. These relationships can occur early in our lives or right now—mentors are personal leaders in our process of personal mastery.

Financial restraint comes easy to me, because my parents were determined to live within their means, and their means were limited for a long time. As a child, I never ate out; in fact, we bought very little at the grocery store. We raised most of the food we ate on my mother's family farm, including animals, fruits and vegetables. Working at the farm on weekends was sometimes backbreaking, and experiences like slaughtering an animal could be scary to a young girl. But because I learned at an young age how to be self-sufficient, few situations frighten me when it comes to providing for myself. I watched my childhood mentors do so, and I participated with them in successful efforts. A history of contributing my best efforts to achieve collective and meaningful success is the root of my confidence. In my work today, I assert that organizations must give their people opportunities to be their best; they can do great things and have meaningful success through a creative and highly participative process.

My family was self-reliant in many other ways, and I was invited to contribute. Until I was in high school, for example, my clothes were made of fabric bought on sale and sewn by my mother, my aunt and me. Even though I realized that I dressed a bit differently than my classmates, I had a sense of empowerment based on the fact that I knew how to find quality fabrics with cool patterns and actually make my own clothes. I don't necessarily think that all children should learn to sew their own clothes, but I believe that every person—every child and every adult—should be given opportunities to create something from nothing. The challenge for leaders is to give people opportunities to invent things that are actually put into use. Work gains immense meaning, and the impact creates stronger individuals, stronger teams, and, ultimately, stronger organizations.

Transformational opportunities are important sustenance, but not all goals are created equal. For example, my frugal parents did not get a telephone until I was 12 years old. I had pined for the chance to call and talk to my friends the way I heard about them calling and talking to each other. To me, getting a phone was a high-priority goal—until we got one. At first, I was thrilled. But after calling my best friend every day after school for six months to talk about boys and exchange gossip, I realized that we had been fine without the phone and its tiresome drain on time and energy. The phone was only a possession. In itself, it was not a reward. And for me it didn't lead to fulfillment. It was exhausting! Today, I'm careful to focus on goals that are not based on things or money but instead are aimed at making a positive difference in the quality of employees' and clients' lives.

Today, I drive the best kind of car ... one that's paid for. My car was not always a high-performance sports coupe, but it was always paid for. Growing up, I was driven around in a 15-year-old Chevy Impala that my father bought for $95 and painted with a paint gun. I had a love-hate relationship with that car. I was a teenager, so of course I thought driving around in a stylish new car would feel great. What stands out about this Chevy, however, is what it meant to my family. We would sit around the dinner table at night and talk about how our family was making progress financially and would one day have enough money saved to buy a house. That's when I loved the Impala. I could see it as a symbol of our power to make choices and our ability to reach for dreams.

Understanding those kitchen-table talks about sticking with the Impala so we could achieve bigger goals is relevant for leadership. Sometimes leaders have a vision of what is possible, but they fail to communicate it. They say something like "We have to do more with less to get where we're going." This statement is true, and it may be enough to motivate the leader, who has a vantage point others do not. But unless the leader can paint a picture of the future secured by sacrifice and can help people align their energies to move toward this vision, they're likely to become disillusioned, demoralized and despondent. It's not enough for leaders to make personal sacrifices.

Many valiantly do more with much less themselves, but they fail to bring their organizations along with them. What they must do is involve everyone in the organizational family in a shared vision and inspire consensus that today's sacrifices are worth tomorrow's payoff.

My family's sacrifices and hard work paid off. In 1976, my parents were finally able to buy a house. Until then, we had lived in cramped but cozy quarters in a small rented duplex. I was 13 years old when we moved. It's hard to relate my excitement the day we moved into that house. I remember the first night we were there as a family—it's etched in my style of leadership. My parents sat us down to talk about how our family's collective sacrifices over the years had paid off. They called up memories, and they acknowledged all the sacrifice and effort everyone had made to advance to that wonderful point. That night, my parents made sure I felt as though I had been part of achieving the goal of buying the house. Today, as a leader, I believe it is very important to go through the iterative process with one's team on a regular basis, collectively going over what was expected and discussing what worked, what didn't work, and why. I believe it's crucial to take the time to acknowledge what went right and the wonderful impact of what individuals and groups have achieved. This process requires intellectual honesty so that participants in the transformation can begin to understand the power of implementation, measurement, inquiry and honest feedback. As the old saying goes, we don't manage what we don't measure.

These are some ways that transformation takes groups and individuals from scarcity to abundance, from shortfall to wholeness, even from sickness to health. The process can be painful and even chaotic. In turbulent times, people look to leaders for a sense of calm and assurance that all will be better if the collective keeps moving forward. These leaders embody possibility. They offer models of discipline, which difficulties require. This truth is easy enough in the abstract, but walking the difficult walk is what gives a leader authenticity when he or she asks others to redouble discipline and approach problems calmly.

My confidence that discipline can outsmart difficulties was born when my family endured its own crisis. Not surprisingly, my parents were underinsured. When my mother suffered a severe, long-term illness that required expensive medical treatments, my father faced not only a personal crisis but also a daunting financial challenge and the added challenge of providing leadership for his children. The memory tells the tale, and what I remember is how, for several years, every month we would all pile into the car on Saturday and drive the 40 minutes to Knoxville so my mother could have the treatment she needed. During the several hours she was in treatment, my father would find ways to entertain us, walking us around the city, stopping at a diner to buy us a soda, and telling us stories and jokes to keep our spirits up. He was tending to our attitudes, using his own attitude and energy to lead us through what might have been a far scarier experience as we waited for our mother to get well.

Our parents were able to lead us by example even as they shouldered burdens we could not understand. My brothers and I recognized our own roles in the family effort to help my mother regain her health. Yes, we were bored on those Saturdays, but we did our best to support the "team" and stay on good behavior. We pitched in to help with the family workload. We cooperated with our father's efforts, and, even though we were children, we appreciated how hard he was trying. We admired him. There's nothing like a leader you can admire. As I have evolved in different circumstances into a leader myself, I often recall the patience I saw my father bring to bear on those Saturday trips. The way he maintained his sense of humor, calm and compassion when things were not optimal created a lasting impression on me. I see in my father's commitment to us some of the most important attributes of a transformational leader.

The commitment my parents embodied and the energy with which they pursued their goals on their family's behalf became guiding lights as I began to venture out to find my own way in the world. Their patience and calm as they shepherded us through the ongoing family transformation became my own, and their compassion inspired the same in me. I was able to draw on their courageous example as I moved into young adulthood and chose to pursue a vision of a way of life far different from anything any of us knew.

Despite the added work it meant at home for other family members, when I turned 16 they all encouraged me to take my first job in a local restaurant as the salad bar attendant. It was time to save money for college. Working inside in a restaurant setting was a novelty to me—I thought I'd died and gone to heaven! Those leaves of lettuce were a lot prettier than any leaves of tobacco I'd come across in the fields. Also, the place was air conditioned, and I never had to pick up a hoe or a tobacco stick to perform my duties. Life was good. When I started, I didn't know exactly how to act or what to do in a restaurant. I had read about restaurants in novels, and I had the little etiquette book my parents had given me when I was much younger as a way to prepare me for life. By observing, I began to learn about how to behave in public. I was beginning to realize that the world was a big place, and I'd need experience and education to thrive. Even today, I don't feel as though I've achieved any final plateau; every day is a chance to learn more and continue developing. This is the seminal challenge for all leaders. For me, it began in earnest in the early days of my first job at the salad bar.

In 1981, I started college at the University of Tennessee in Knoxville, putting myself through school by working two or three part-time jobs at a time. Although the family work ethic remained strong, punctuality and discipline suffered when I first went away to college. Thanks to the ever-present influence of my mother, I had been a serious student in high school—I made good grades and was always punctual. However, in my freshman year, I was late for almost every class and put off my homework assignments until the last minute. Needless to say, this lack of time management was reflected in my grades. It wasn't until the following summer that I realized I had to take charge of my life. I bought my first day planner and began an ongoing quest to make the most of my time. From this experience, I learned how important it is to internalize the lessons and wisdom imparted by our mentors, to make them our own. Mentors (like my mother) can only point me in the right direction. Their influence comes and goes in my life. In the end, I'm left to master my own decisions and choices.

I was enthralled by the wide variety of subjects in my college coursework. Thanks to a wonderful professor, Dr. Michael Gordon, I was most drawn to industrial psychology. He saw my potential and challenged me by pointing out that I had talent that could make a difference in the world. His words of encouragement shaped the way my life was moving forward. I'm still in contact with Michael Gordon to this day. As a leader, I realize that every thought, word and deed counts in every interaction. I'm careful about what I project, realizing that people can be influenced to a much greater extent than you might think by the energy and actions of leaders. I encourage leaders to be vigilant about the impact they can have on the world by making a difference in one person's life.

After graduation, I worked for a year as the distribution coordinator for programs aired by a communications company. But my hunger for learning led me back to academia. In 1986, I moved to Virginia to immerse myself in the industrial-organizational psychology graduate program at Virginia Tech. I had a lot of fun conducting research in the areas of leader emergence; the impact of natural bias on performance appraisals conducted by leaders; and the impact of leader-subordinate relations on motivation, satisfaction and other organizational factors. Although designing and conducting research was hard work, my mentor, Dr. Roseanne Foti, made it seem like the most important and fascinating thing I could be doing. Roseanne had a profound impact on my early career. She showed me how to make the hard work and effort of transformation as much fun as possible. We remain close to this day and serve together on a National Science Foundation grant promoting interdisciplinary graduate research.

As a doctoral intern, I had the opportunity to live in Atlanta, Georgia, working in the Human Resources Research Division of Bell-South Corporation. The internship gave me valuable exposure to the corporate world, both its challenges and its disciplines. The energy and sense of possibility I experienced at BellSouth convinced me that I belonged in that setting, either as an employee or a consultant. I returned to Virginia Tech to complete my final exams and dissertation, and earned a doctorate in industrial and organizational psychology in 1993. It hadn't been a cakewalk, but I'd made it through and was thrilled to be starting my career at the age of 30. I returned to the corporate world. Within a year, like my father, I launched a business.

Every day I'm honored to serve many leaders as they seek to create cultures of transformation in their organizations. Individual self-discipline clarifies and energizes the work of people in commercial enterprises, and those in nonprofit and government agencies as well. I'm especially struck by how well our military clients already understand that leadership begins with a disciplined mastery of oneself. I've worked in most sectors of the economy, and experience has shown me that leaders everywhere have much in common. They summon the best they have to become the best they can be.

We can be mentors to each other, and we can inspire new levels of leadership in ourselves and those around us. We can take the need for continuous transformation in the world personally by mastering ourselves first. Our personal mastery can enrich our mastery of interpersonal dynamics and networks. With clarity, commitment and energy, you can lead your organization into a bright future—one decision at a time.

CHAPTER ONE

Snapshot

Imagining the Transformational Leader in You

Books about leaders often have photos of leaders in action. A biography of Sir Winston Churchill inevitably shows him with a stogie in his mouth, walking along Downing Street. A chronicle of Abraham Lincoln's life invariably includes haunting portraits that don't capture the humor he brought to managing the rivals in his cabinet. This book, too, seems to warrant a "snapshot," because it is about leaders, up close and personal, drawing on their own stories to advance themselves and those around them. I'm talking about stories of transformation.

My snapshot will rely on words to carry an image of what this book can help you do. It's the "picture" of a leader who has no blind, unenergized followers, but who is so much about unleashing the full potential of an organization that he draws out the leadership potential of everyone who is contributing to the goals of transformation and participating in achieving measurable results. This picture is of a leader who can create the calm, powerful force that makes people actively seek leadership while simultaneously shining their own lights.

Many people operate under the false assumption that leadership is an innate talent. The success of my clients demonstrates that leadership is a very high-level skill that can be cultivated and mastered over time. I've seen great executives discover and mentor new generations of leaders, even as they move their groups to unimagined levels of achievement. As their enterprise grows, they benefit from having cultivated executive talent to handle the many new opportunities that come with success. That's what this snapshot is about: a leader in motion, transforming to meet the challenges of today's new world realities.

What is the image of the person this book is encouraging into being?

Leaders can be anyone, very much like you or me, who simply remains vigilant. They are people who embrace their imperfections, growing wise by learning from and building on their mistakes. To them, problems are not obstacles but exciting opportunities to be seized. Despite pressure, they've learned to remain focused and clear, and their calm confidence sets the tone for everyone around them. Time is not the enemy; it's just another resource, a precious resource, to be used well and managed as carefully as any inventory or project. Before they push others to new levels of performance, leaders are already pushing themselves. They don't settle for anything but the right information to guide and shape sound decisions. They are not restless, but they will not rest until they see results.

Leaders are authentic and credible. They mind their manners in every encounter with every person. That makes them fair and respectful. People do not feel used by them, but tapped and challenged and supported. That is in large part because leaders take genuine pleasure in groups of people and do not recoil from someone who needs to share feelings or voice dissent. Their sense of fairness leads to unity and mutual respect among everyone around them. Diversity in the workforce is yet another resource for new ideas and creative possibility. It becomes easy—in fact, it becomes fun—to join forces with others and work collaboratively toward a greater, shared goal. It's been said many times that people don't care what you know until they know that you care. Leaders care not only about the goal but also about the people heading toward it.

Of all the habits I've observed in leaders, listening is the rarest skill of a masterful leader, along with simply being quiet. Breakthroughs at meetings cannot occur if a leader is talking nonstop.

Resolutions among smart people who are passionate about their work cannot occur if they don't all have a way to voice their point of view. Without the calm, powerful force unique to mature leaders, dynamic energy cannot be released to power an enterprise forward into sustainable success. Balancing the need for decisions with the many benefits of patience, leaders work and live in such a way that their own guiding principles and values light the path for an entire organization.

I encourage you to keep this snapshot in mind as we explore the process of developing the personal mastery needed to emerge as a leader in the ever more competitive global economy that is our new home.

Integrity

Unleash the Greatest Force for Success

I ntegrity influences the type of success you can achieve. This is why I believe any book about leadership must discuss integrity from the start.

A leader who is committed to integrity promotes the freedom to contribute one's best, which includes the likelihood that there will be mistakes on the way to achieving excellence and sustaining a culture of transformation and creativity. All our clients operate at the highest levels of leadership with unrivaled integrity. One reason they trust our counsel is because we share the view that integrity is essential to leadership. We transform organizations into dynamic cultures of motivated professionals, but we start by assuming that leaders with integrity are the key ingredient.

We believe integrity is the practical, basic building block. It is essential to success. It is not something a few lucky leaders can afford—those who don't have to deal with the free-for-all of a competitive global market, in which most others are trying to find a way to be one of the fittest who will survive. On the contrary, we believe that integrity makes or breaks real success in that very marketplace.

But before we proceed with an entire book based on the concept of integrity, let's first challenge our assumption that a person must have it to lead. Otherwise, we could be accused of having a Pollyanna view of business, when, in fact, ours is a real-world program with real-world results.

One way I test my assumptions is to open a dialog with the smartest people I know. As I was writing this chapter, I decided to invite comments using a tool that demonstrates the radical way advancing technologies and the virtual work world are connecting people across industries and nations. I turned to my favorite online professional network of highly accomplished thought and business leaders. I posted this question about the relationship between integrity and leadership: *Is integrity critical for successful leadership?* The question hit a nerve. This network includes high-level experts with extremely busy schedules; they normally reply over a period of days or even weeks. Consider my surprise when the responses came pouring in within the first hour!

Glenn Curry, partner of Efficient Technologies, LLC, wrote first, challenging the idea with an acute sense of observation and justice: "Leaders with integrity? I would venture them to be more the exception than the rule. Although it is nice to assert honesty, integrity and other positive behaviors and values as being attributes of leadership, there is no such requirement. In fact, it would be easier for someone lacking them to grab control and take over leadership. . . . " Robert Poulk, operations engineer, MCSE, Certified PM, agreed, writing, "History is full of successful leaders who were also scoundrels, e.g., Hitler, Stalin, any number of Roman emperors. . . . "

The dialog was off and running.

Everyone agreed that integrity was an admirable, even desirable, trait in leaders and in people generally, but many stopped short of agreeing with Hamish Taylor, a consultant and coach for Shinergise Partners, Ltd. (Scotland), who wrote, "Leaders who lose their integrity lose their right to lead. They might as well go and play online poker for the rest of their professional careers!"

In the dialog, numerous leaders shared the sentiment of Kathryn Alexander, president of Ethical Impact, Inc., who wrote, "Wouldn't it be wonderful if unethical and dishonest actions didn't work? Of course a person can be unethical and also be 'successful.'" Ann Carr, owner and principal of Ann Attayek Carr and Associates, LLC, wrote, "I am sad to report that the 'right answer' is actually 'No, they do not have to have integrity to be successful leaders.' I base this on the observation that lots of execs are actually pretty successful with quite a low or no level of integrity."

However, a certain thread began to emerge that gets at why TSI considers integrity crucial for successful leadership. Juha Härkönen, chief operating officer of TELLUS International, Inc., wrote, "If your only measure of success is monetary, then you do not need integrity to succeed, but that success doesn't often repeat." Steven Walker, organization development manager at Credit Suisse, wrote, "An executive must have integrity to be successful over the long term. It's a prerequisite."

Stephanie G. Seay, senior editor with Platts, a division of the McGraw-Hill Companies, reflected, "Integrity seems relative these days. When CEOs are increasingly pressured by Wall Street analysts continually to produce more and more profit, to cut costs while growing revenues year after year in order to gain a favorable rating by those analysts who influence investors, then issues that I personally associate with integrity (such as treatment of employees and respect for the environment) are often pushed to the side. If integrity is keeping your word to business associates, clients or customers, then it is essential in order to maintain trust in these relationships and grow your business. When you join an organization whose goal is to make money, then ruthlessness may be more highly valued than integrity. So I suppose it depends on what kind of organization you lead as to whether you'll actually have much *allowance* for integrity."

Conversely, executives who are in a position to compare and contrast diverse companies as possible employers will decide whether a company keeps its word and otherwise treats employees with integrity or whether it is ruthless and not committed to developing any talent beyond that needed to survive a hostile environment. By their choice, they will, in a sense vote. This is the kind of choice organizations present before they ever recruit—or develop—leadership. Organizations that project integrity attract and reward integrity in their leadership.

Managers who find themselves in leadership positions do not need help from TSI to create a short-term windfall at the expense of the long-term health of their organizations. That kind of success is, relatively speaking, easy to achieve. These professionals can be called "leaders," and these managers who occupy leadership positions can define or accept goals with a narrow scope. Enron is almost-mythic proof of how that kind of success is impossible to sustain. Think of the crumbling empires throughout history that could not sustain an endless series of conquests, and you can see that some national leaders failed to establish long-term stability. Their strategy lacked integrity. The scope of their vision was not challenged by a sense of integrity; it was limited to narrow and inflexible goals. In contrast, our clients seek TSI counsel for organizational transformation precisely because they know that the environment in which they operate demands flexibility and success at every level. They need to create stable, competitive organizations so they can sustain success.

As the dialog of leaders continued, Tracy Saunders, owner of Intruequest, touched on the key relationship TSI focuses on in developing leaders. Saunders wrote, "In terms of sustainability, integrity is a requirement for followership. Without followers, there are no leaders." Allen Laudenslager, a freelance writer and trainer, took the point further, saying that "most leaders of a team are members of a higher level team" who have to be flexible enough to be followers sometimes. Jennifer M. Whitlock, president and CEO of Totemic Business Solutions, LLC, wrote, "Executives are only as good as the team they lead. Executives with high integrity will often gain the respect of their employees." Together, the leader and those who work for her create a culture, and that culture is what determines whether goals are met; in fact, culture can greatly influence what goals are set in the first place.

I usually take this idea a step further with my clients: Like attracts like. Not only do employees respect a leader with integrity, but employees who have integrity themselves are drawn to this kind of leader. The culture of the organization does follow the leader, but it is also based on the day-to-day relationships among all the people who contribute their talent, expertise and energy. That's why culture determines achievements. This is one way the leader's integrity influences the type of success that can be achieved. It determines the kind of people who are drawn to contribute to the leader's vision and goals.

An example from James Potter, head of sales and marketing for BASIS Limited (United Kingdom), makes this point clear: "... if an employee told a personal detail issue to a leader with integrity, he would be consultative, counseling and trying to help the employee. On the flip side, the leader with no integrity would share the information with colleagues, use it for leverage, etc. I know which leader I would choose and which one is most likely to build a team that trusts and values and supports the leader and the business." Multiply this instance by many, and consider how employees watch leaders, observing how they treat their colleagues and judging them by what they see.

When employees value integrity and are led by an executive who creates a trusting and supportive culture, they are more likely to contribute freely—even to extend themselves. By contrast, when people work for an executive who does not have integrity, they often hold back on what they invest in the organization. Instead, they may use their talents to find new positions, and the best talent is often the first to leave. This process cripples an organization. Terri L. Maurer, founder and president of the Maurer Consulting Group, made the point, writing, "To be a leader, one must have followers. Without integrity, followers will drop by the wayside, leaving the leader leading himself or herself and trying to get the job done with little support." That's a formula for failure.

The risks are clear. Michael Aitken, general manager for community services, Christchurch City Council (New Zealand), wrote, "All of this comes to nothing without integrity. Although one can still have compliant staff, such leaders are a long way from having an *engaged* staff. Without having an engaged staff, whatever success the business is having, it is still not reaching its potential." Even more to the point, Andrew Lyde, vice president of the Center for Courageous Enterprise, wrote, "Fortunately or unfortunately, leaders are successful when those who follow make them successful."

When TSI starts working with a new client, our first line of inquiry is about what's being done to tap the full potential of the organization and those who contribute to its success. For an organization to compete in the high-tech global market, it must tap the full potential of all its resources, including its human resources. People cannot be just compliant followers—the type that leaders without integrity require. Success requires fully empowered contributors, people who support the leader who supports them.

This dynamic is most apparent in today's military. History tells us that many innovations first appeared and were tested in military settings. And new technologies and historic shifts in the nature of warfare require more and more capacity for exercising independent thought under fire—to follow is often a matter of knowing when to lead. Throughout history, our military has distinguished itself through all the known and unsung heroes who were not only willing to obey orders but were also able to step into unanticipated leadership roles when circumstances suddenly shifted. To master this balance of independence and cooperation, the military has always been an organization of leaders who follow. The need for integrity is undisputed in this environment, where everyone's life depends on collective trust and support. Many of our clients are military or military-trained. These leaders know the crucial importance of an inviolate chain of command to survive in the heat of battle. As they move into the future, they draw on that experience while also continuously reaffirming the need to foster independence and self-mastery and to define leadership as being first among equals.

Our business clients know what our military clients know—that integrity is critical for success even after the crisis of conflict has passed. Many organizations must adjust for the long haul, the test of endurance after the crisis. Commercial, government or nonprofit—all organizations understand this concept: Coping with short-term challenges and managing for sustained success are the two halves of the business cycle. What has changed is what is always changing: the business environment. From now on, the environment will be a global one, subject to many more unpredictable forces. Competition for resources and the need for cost containment require us to use resources in streamlined ways at full-steam force. Advances in technology continue unabated, demanding flexible and growth-oriented people and systems. Whether short-term or long-term, our success depends more and more on a well-balanced business culture, which in turn depends on its leadership, which must function with integrity to motivate its talent to their full potential.

As Tracy Saunders wrote, "Without followers, there are no leaders." The opposite is also true: Without leaders, there are no followers. Organizations must transform into versatile and dynamic groups. In this transformation, leadership can no longer be limited to outdated definitions in which a person can find herself in a leadership position and be expected to lead without the support of everyone around her. Leadership is shared. It may pass to others for short periods of time.

In fact, in this new vision of leadership, I'll go so far as to assert that there are no followers. There are leaders and there are people who contribute at their maximum potential. They don't need to waste energy watching their backs, because the leader's integrity sets the tone for a trusting and supportive environment. This is a workplace well worth transforming into.

CHAPTER THREE

Personal Mastery

Access Spirit and Energy for Change

W hen an organization must change course, it is often assumed that the first step is to change the course of the organization. That seems obvious. And it's right—or half right.

My career has been devoted to helping leaders shepherd organizations through radical change—and toward outstanding successes. It doesn't matter whether a client is with a commercial business, a government agency, or a not-for-profit association, he will need to strategically tap and deploy all resources if he wants a maximum outcome with minimal risk. The work of transformation transcends industry type—all leaders face similar obstacles to change. Often, the first obstacle is incorrect assumptions. For example, some people look for a shortcut to transformation. Others believe they can limit change to small groups—or even individuals—as they seek results that only authentic, continuous transformation can deliver. Both ideas are misguided and are sure to disappoint.

A culture of transformation requires serious effort and single-minded commitment. That's the only way to achieve authentic change and lasting results. I discourage clients from starting this process unless they truly want a self-perpetuating culture of ongoing transformation. Sometimes people need to learn by failure. It takes some groups time to get to the point where they are willing to commit the resources and energy to transform into a success story.

When a client needs a quick fix for an immediate problem, TSI can help with stopgap measures. However, when we enter into a paid client engagement, we do everything we can to ensure that our services promote the client's self-reliance quickly. Our work, even in a crisis situation, leads to preparing the client for future challenges. Leaders come to us because they know their organizations must change, sometimes very fast. But even in difficult circumstances, they trust our counsel against making their first step a direct dive into the business of limited, harried change. Our clients have enough passion for their organizations that they are willing to start the transformation from the inside out. They're willing to take stock and, in light of current obstacles and opportunities, master themselves anew.

Leadership lies at the core of an organization's success. It determines what kinds of people are available to contribute to the organization's achievements and how freely those people can contribute the best of themselves to the outcome. Regardless of how much expertise and competence are present in any group, it's the leadership that determines how much that power is tapped and how energetic the group dynamic can be. Change in leadership must precede organizational change. And change in leadership relies on individual leaders seeking personal transformation and, in the process, inspiring, modeling, driving and guiding change around them. That is *authentic* organizational change.

Change in leadership is rarely about the dramatic turns of events when leaders are ousted or resign. Most leaders are no less committed than a captain to his vessel, and are willing and able to evolve right along with their organizations through any rough waters or difficult turnabouts. The challenge is how to change, and the wisdom lies in figuring out how to change *first*, before you lead the organization in a new direction. If at all possible, a prudent captain does not sail the ship into uncharted waters.

Leaders have a choice.

If you picked up this book, you're a leader. If someone handed you this book, it's because they think you're a leader or they're challenging you to expand your leadership potential. You may have your doubts about your leadership qualities, but I assure you that regardless of whether divisions report to you or you're a solitary expert working in your specialized field, you will be called upon to exercise leadership in the economy of tomorrow. In a market that is increasingly global, competitive, high-speed and high-tech, no one will be a professional island and almost everyone will have to contribute at a level of personal awareness that was once reserved for leaders.

This is why I encourage you to start the transformation with yourself, to embark on (or continue) a process of personal mastery. If you expect a team of talented professionals to master their expertise and contribute to a shared goal, you must master your own expertise, not just as a leading force but as a unifying force as well. If you expect the organization to tap its full potential, you must tap your own full potential as a leader who can inspire and energize, not just direct and organize. In other words, the starting point for organizational transformation is you. Master yourself to be your best, to do great things, and to have meaningful success.

I'm careful when I talk about personal mastery to clients, who are generally very high achievers and driven to fix problems. If a client gets the idea that she is the obstacle to progress in the organization, she'll immediately reach for a pen and paper and start listing faults to fix. A problem solver at heart, she won't hesitate to embrace a program to "fix" anything, including herself. But when you want to lead an organization into transformation, it's not about transforming yourself into something different. It's about being more—more of who you authentically are.

Listing and fixing our faults is a process that works about as well as enrolling in a gym on January 2nd. Many gyms count on the fact that visits from the vast majority of new members will taper off within a few months; most facilities are not built to handle the strain of everyone's New Year's resolutions. The same scenario often plays out with regard to plans for organizational change. After paying big bucks for big specialists to present big theories, many organizations shelve big plans for big change after a short time, because the structure and culture of the organization simply cannot cope with the strain of the transformation on a day-to-day basis. Many of these plans were good plans with excellent goals. But, the first step was skipped, and anything that followed was bound to founder.

If you want a plan to secure long-term, sustainable success, you must understand that before the plan comes you.

This may seem confusing: The first step to transforming an organization is about *you*. But it isn't about fixing you—or the organization. As I often tell my clients, fix-it efforts are hard to sustain, either by you or by those who will be following you through transformational change. That's because a fix-it trajectory has to keep finding negative things to fix. When fault-fixing becomes part of your organization's new culture, it can quickly run amok, draining the energy from your best contributors. It rewards a negative focus and de-motivates the people on whom you depend. Energy is drained from work life just when the group dynamic should be energized by its efforts. Fixing faults can become a formidable obstacle to the change you wanted in the first place. So don't start this process by focusing on fixing the organization's faults or your own. Embark on a path toward personal mastery.

Personal mastery is a far more positive approach to inspiring change, welcoming change, fostering change and sustaining change —change in yourself and then change in all those around you. It's a positive approach to life. For leadership to be consistently effective, you can't force it. You must constantly evolve and share that evolution with those around you. For the impact of your leadership to be enduring, you can't fake it. Leadership must be authentic to inspire people to take the risks involved in changing course. Seeking personal mastery before you turn to group dynamics and the enterprise itself will project that you walk the walk before you talk the talk.

Your success as a leader relies on practicing personal mastery not as if it were a one-hour commitment to jog or to meditate each day but as a choice to evolve every day toward higher levels of ability. We're not talking about getting an A+ in class or breaking a habit or getting a makeover. Classes end, habits can be forgotten, makeovers come undone. But life and its challenges continue unabated.

Personal mastery is about life. Life is open-ended, surprising and challenging, and so is personal mastery. Life thrives on imagination, vision and commitment. So does the world in which you and your organization can thrive. So, the first real step toward transforming your organization is to grasp a working concept of what personal mastery really is—and make a commitment to a renewed way of life as a leader.

Personal mastery ultimately puts you in charge of yourself. Our military clients understand this idea immediately, and many of our commercial and nonprofit leaders instinctively believe it, even though they may not have experienced basic training or the heat of battle, where personal mastery is put to the ultimate test and where every person leads in some way.

As you master yourself for the new direction you envision for your organization, you first develop a comfortable awareness of your own internal states, preferences, impulses, goals and sense of purpose. Then you realize there is constant flux and change. The picture is not less accurate if it varies from day to day. *You* vary from day to day. Your business and its environment vary from day to day. The question is whether you understand the variations well enough to use them to master the challenges that come your way. As you become more open to opportunities and challenges, and practice new and consciously chosen reactions, your blind spots and weaknesses diminish.

Your self-worth is grounded in self-knowledge. You have clear reasons to be confident, and equally clear reasons for caution as you work with your weaknesses. Your capacity for adapting to an ever-changing world is a foundation on which to build. Your readiness for new opportunities and ideas is focused and energized. You become the living example of what you want people around you to be, and what your organization must be to thrive.

The process of personal mastery forces us to do what most people have a very hard time doing—assessing ourselves as more than the sum of a list of faults. As our focus broadens, the accuracy of our self-assessment will improve, and our ability to assess the organization and its capabilities will also improve.

Of course, in addition to our talents and strengths, we do identify weaknesses. But in the context of personal mastery, some faults turn out to be nothing more than strengths that have not been fully developed.

The question is not how to get rid of them but how to harness their full power. Some faults disappear, not because we wrestle with them but because we strengthen other parts of ourselves. Even failures become part of a cycle of learning and tools for advancing in knowledge and ability. Failures become part of eventual success. We seek balance, not reduction.

The hardest part of facing our weaknesses is understanding that they are starting points for change. They can evolve if we work to transform ourselves. Weaknesses are not excuses any more. The common excuse for avoiding change—I can't do it!—is replaced by something more honest and more possible. Transformation has become the imperative.

Authenticity

Leadership is about the choice to be authentic. Popping a pill to temporarily relieve a symptom is easier than working to create holistic health. It's the same with leadership: Unless you do the work, you can only hope to project an image; you can't actually lead. And without your full commitment to lead, some portion of the full potential of the organization will remain dormant. In today's environment, that's not an option.

Managers in leadership positions sometimes cling to their comfort zones—working at what they already know how to do creates the illusion of effectiveness. Meanwhile, the organization is evolving, and the old range of competency is not enough. These managers keep trying to solve new problems with old methods. They move into entirely new circumstances using yesterday's work modes. What they're really doing is resisting change. Their leadership lacks authenticity. It is ineffective because it resists the truth about changing circumstances.

Sometimes, the least effective thing to do is to do what you know. Mastering yourself is a commitment to what you do not entirely know about yourself; it will lead you into more and more untapped potential, which you can experience only with time and effort. Unless you're willing to truly learn about yourself—and then about the people and the organization around you—you cannot grow. And if you cannot grow, you cannot change.

Leaders sometimes seem to turn a blind eye to their own foibles while they spend time identifying the problems around them. We must be willing to change our work habits, our areas of expertise, and our relationships with others. We must become open to everything around us if we want to lead others to meaningful success. We must endure the discomfort of dealing with personal symptoms to achieve a new level of organizational health. Once we begin a quest for personal mastery, however, our efforts will start to lead change. Our leadership becomes more authentic. Instead of finding faults to fix, we look for potential to cultivate. Everything we do inspires others to do the same. We personify the success to which we are leading. Our leadership has become authentic.

Rear Admiral Grace Hopper was a management expert whose practical wisdom was refined during the years she served as one of the first female admirals in the U.S. Navy. Hopper once observed that the difference between being a leader and a manager is largely one of choice. She watched as managers, when faced with pressure, worked ably with processes, models and systems. Tasks got done, but groups remained without direction. Leaders, on the other hand, not only exhibited competence and expertise but also were committed to the group's process. Leaders invested their time working with people and their emotions. They took time to elicit cooperation, to listen to individuals, and to place the needs of others above their own. Work was accomplished, and the teams cultivated in the process were better able to handle the next wave of work. Leaders behaved in a way that transformed the group.[1]

Most of us have leadership attitudes and behaviors. All of us have the potential to be leaders. Choice determines what happens to our potential. I remind clients that they already possess all the qualities they need to initiate and sustain change. They just have to choose to make these qualities their own, to practice these attitudes and behaviors consistently, day after day. That's how we become more than managers in positions of authority. We become authentic leaders.

An authentic leader is the sum of competence and authenticity; however, when we're stuck, we often revert to using only half of the equation to get to the solution. Every time we rely on competence alone to solve a problem, we limit ourselves. We are simply managing.

Our scope is narrow; our vision limited. It's hard for people to follow a colleague who is frozen in that state of mind.

Authentic leaders know they're not likely to make progress over the long haul simply by managing. Competence is an attribute in anyone who contributes to the outcome. But it is a tool, not a direction. Sometimes, it's not even a conscious process. Progress requires more. It requires evolution, choice and discipline. Because leadership relies on groups of people working together, it requires authenticity.

"Authenticity" is harder to define and quantify than "competence," but it is crucial for leadership. A person may be competent, but we've all heard of the executive who clings to his desk, doing the work without knowing how to engage others. This executive is usually surrounded by disgruntled employees. Disappointment and resentment permeate a work environment with an unwilling leader at the helm, because people want to be tapped. They want to contribute. They want to be committed. They want leadership.

Authenticity is reflected in personal commitment in two areas. First, we need to understand ourselves better. We must grow conscious of ourselves and be ourselves rather than trying to be what we think a leader should look like. Second, we must commit to changing old habits, such as how we think, what we value, how we work, how we connect with people, how we manage frustration, how we learn, and what we expect from life. As we do this, we'll see less projection and more transparency. There will be little posturing, little that is hidden or mysterious. Authenticity permits clarity.

To be authentic is to be intelligent in a whole new way, one that moves beyond competence and creates direction. The more authentic we are, the more spontaneously we can move among competent persons who seek our direction. The capacity for this intelligence lies within us all. So, who will end up being the leader? You will, if you choose.

Honesty

Most of our clients hear the word "honesty" and feel pretty comfortable. They generally have not lied, and they usually have long careers where straight shooting has been valued. In other words, they've been good leaders. However, they can become impeccable leaders in motion, driving a culture of transformation forward to unimagined achievements. For that, even honest leaders must dive deeper to new levels of honesty.

The hardest person to be honest with is oneself. The leaders who can launch and sustain an organizational transformation are those who can readily admit their failures and offer insights into lessons learned. They are emotionally detached from any judgment of them selves. What matters is not their self-image or hiding from embarrassing facts; they are single-mindedly pursuing the progress of the enterprise. They are, in a word, a little more *fearless* than other leaders. It takes courage to choose to be honest about ourselves.

Managers who step into a leadership role are not necessarily opposed to being honest with themselves. Many of those who see the need for change are willing to focus on whatever can be changed, even if it includes their own habits or performance. The question is whether you believe there is a need to seek a deeper level of honesty with yourself before you evaluate the problems in the organization. It can be surprising how much even a maverick is wired to resist change in new circumstances.

In fact, any of us can resist change—even change we desire. In the early stages, when we're planning change, a common falsehood can hobble our vision and all progress that follows afterward. We tell ourselves a dangerous untruth—that some things, including things about ourselves, need not or simply cannot change. We don't tell these untruths on purpose; in fact, we don't even notice them, because the beliefs have become part of the landscape. So, for a leader, honesty means not just questioning assumptions at work around us; it means looking for assumptions we're not even aware of. These are usually things we believe about ourselves.

This kind of honesty requires us to question all our foregone conclusions. We need to challenge ourselves about anything we assume cannot change and be vigilant about outdated assumptions. Sometimes it helps to get counsel from people outside the organization, so we're not asking the people we're inviting to change to help *us* change as well. Clarity about what's going on inside sometimes comes best from the outside. Mentors and trusted confidantes can be a valuable part of the mix as we push ourselves toward more fearless self-awareness.

One way to identify an unexamined falsehood at work is to look for the excuses we make to ourselves. Excuses can be a way of resisting change. It takes a whole new level of honesty to say that your weaknesses are not an excuse to hold back—or a reason to beat yourself up. This concept is easy to write about but hard to put into practice. But if you want to lead an organization through change, you're going to have to tackle its false barriers. And how can you do that authentically if you're not tackling your own?

Another way leaders undermine themselves is by focusing only on weaknesses and failures—or on a single achievement. If we're honest and fair with ourselves, we must consider ourselves in the context of our whole person. Until we do that, what we have to offer will be incomplete. And what we are able to see in those around us and in our environments will be similarly limited.

Being honest with staff earns their trust. It's an example of integrity at work in communications. And being honest with yourself increases your trust in yourself, in your judgment and your decisions. We need to operate with the clear idea that shortcomings are not permanent inabilities but, rather, undeveloped areas. They do not benefit from obsession or criticism, and they can evolve into strengths with the right attention. Integrity is as important for personal mastery as it is for interpersonal relations. Without it, personal mastery is not really possible. Integrity and self-honesty create a sense of calm and ease, which are among the ineffable characteristics that draw us intuitively to leaders. That's why the first step in personal mastery is choosing honesty. Leaders expect it of themselves and welcome it in those who will be contributing to the end result. Honesty is the antidote for fear.

Consciousness

Leadership involves not just the decision to change but, more important, a commitment to evolve. It's a state of being alive, awake and alert. It's about vigilance. Evolution is not random change. It is change with a specific trajectory in a particular direction. Events and opportunities appear as the direction unfolds. Evolution creates order.

Organizational transformation is evolutionary, and leaders can guide this evolution through their choices. Some choices are actually unconscious reactions, governed by unacknowledged assumptions or emotions. But as a leader exercises more personal mastery, the choices become more conscious. Conscious choices can steer an organization in the right direction.

The more fully people are aware of an organization's direction, the more they can align their own choices with that direction. Many decisions are made about diverse matters every day, and even the best-written memo isn't enough to communicate the need to choose change over and over again. The fastest way to communicate this trajectory is for the leader to consciously choose it herself and—before she gives instructions or directives—live it herself day after day. Leaders must master the evolutionary process in themselves first. To do so, they must become conscious.

This is especially true for leaders who seek to spearhead organizational transformation. They can't change everything with the flip of a switch. Every day they must make choices that channel the energy around them in a common direction. A list of actions can't reorient a group of people into a new trajectory. In the evolutionary process, change is communicated by the way the leader leads.

Transformation relies on conscious choice. Choice starts change. Conscious choice starts conscious change. Choice must cooperate with change. It can guide change. It ensures that change continues as a way of life.

In many ways, change has a bad rap, which is one reason why transforming an organization is a daunting prospect. Too many choices are made by habit, or through inaction, or with blinders on. These are unconscious choices, and they lead to directionless change. Change for the sake of change is not sustainable.

With our clients, we emphasize the fact that a person is free to choose only positive change and a positive direction. In fact, one of TSI's key contributions to organizational transformation is helping our clients discriminate between negative and positive change, and then choose consciously. To make the right choices, leaders must be conscious—of ourselves, our relationships and our environment. We must cultivate consciousness.

Consciousness is not a task that can be completed or checked off on a To Do list. It cannot be acquired once and for all. Consciousness is far more than understanding one person or one process. It's a state of being, a way of life. Consciousness is a cornerstone in the process of personal mastery.

We must choose to be conscious and to stay conscious. Consciousness is a daily commitment that happens one decision at a time. To be conscious is to be alive, awake and alert. A good example of being conscious is skiing down a mountainside at high speed. The skier is vigilant and responsive to the contours and obstacles in the environment. The success of the run relies on alertness and awareness, even as it heightens the ability to be awake and alert. There is a circularity of energy.

Consciousness is a way of being especially alive—some people use the word "mindfulness." It is a state of being that we must choose again and again. We must cultivate our consciousness over time. As it flourishes, we benefit more and more from its effect on the evolutionary trajectory of our lives—professionally and personally. We become better "life skiers," progressing toward the double-diamond slopes with greater skill and relaxed confidence.

Consciousness tends to attract people. Superiors and subordinates alike are drawn to us and trust us. It builds and enriches a social network—the more conscious we are, the more confidence we feel in group settings. However, leaders tend to cultivate consciousness when they are detached—either literally, in time away from the organization, or figuratively, usually by listening without judgment.

This is one of the ways we can use the solitude of leadership to create better leadership, by drawing into a private space to observe, consider and wonder. We use consciousness to improve our ability to imagine. It is central to the energy of creativity.

In a separate space, we become aware of ourselves, our relationships and the organizations we're part of. In this space, we are able to strike a balance among all the demands and rewards. When we've mastered that balance, we emerge at a high-functioning level of leadership. The development of consciousness is the foundation of personal mastery. It is the core of all leadership success.

Our choices today will determine our future; but despite their far-reaching impact, these choices often play out as mundane daily decisions. Consider how small courtesies create lasting goodwill among colleagues. A person can become a powerful catalyst simply by developing the habit of asking others if they need help and, if they do, providing it. A simple "thank you" can punctuate the daily momentum with an important moment of conscious recognition, enriching the bonds on which we rely for organizational success. In the same way, seemingly small individual choices bring great visions into reality and sometimes even change reality and the future.

But conscious evolution usually doesn't start with a great vision. It starts with an idea, and it relies on our willingness to be heretical. Consider Michael Dell. He didn't start with a clear plan to create an 18 billion dollar corporation that employs 25,000 people, or to become the youngest CEO in history of a Fortune 500 company. The clarity of his leadership was reflected in his vision to sell customized computers directly to customers. He drove down the price of computers by using cheap surplus parts and eliminating the middleman.[2]

This vision was heretical in an economy that relied on retail distribution, but Dell and his partners didn't shrink from charting a new direction—and changing the face of the marketplace. Day after day, he made decisions that kept his company on track. These daily decisions, the vision they served, and the intention they carried through created a phenomenon that contributed to the evolution of knowledge and of business. In fact, they changed the course of history.

We, too, can consciously contribute to the evolution of the cultures that dominate our lives, our workplaces, and our world. Confident in their competence, leaders who are called upon to become cultural heretics do not recoil from implementing ideas that challenge the dogma of their industries. In most cases, they don't foresee the transformations they will spark, but they don't shrink from pursuing their vision with one smart choice after another. They live the evolution and survive the challenge by relying on abilities far greater than just how-to skills.

Evolution is under way. Are you aware of the process? Do you want to contribute to the flow? There are cultural heretics all around us—

transforming government, technology, private industry, education and defense. Every sector has its heretics. Every sector needs them.

Be one.

Impact

Our evolution into ever more authentic leaders is a response to what surrounds us. Yet, there is a circularity of energy, because as we evolve into better leaders, we will have a greater impact on our surroundings. We find that the endeavors and the lives connected to ours can move farther with us than alone, and the world that interacts with ours is energized by us and is capable of greater achievements.

Our evolution proceeds one choice at a time. It's hard to imagine the lifelong impact of a single conscious choice, but choices lead to turning points, and each turning point unleashes opportunities we could never have imagined. If we're alert to the new environment even as we help fashion it, we can have a remarkable impact. And it all begins with small changes in a process of personal mastery.

One of my inspirations is Dr. Alfred E. Mann, who understands how conscious contributions, made one step at a time, can greatly advance knowledge and change and can push us to ever higher levels of achievement. In 1999, the House Ear Institute bestowed its highest award, the Humanitarian of the Year Award, on Mann, who is CEO and chairman of the board of MannKind Corporation, a diversified biopharmaceutical company focused on developing novel therapeutics. Mann received the award for the development of an ear implant that restores hearing in people who are deaf. He was feted by luminaries in his field offering speeches in his honor, but it was a four-year-old girl who handed him the award. She had once been deaf. She came onto the stage and simply said, "Thank you, Mr. Mann, for my implant." Later, in an interview, he tearfully recalled, "It was the most moving thing you can ever imagine."

Mann's discovery changed the lives of many people, but he went further by choosing to invest in the advance of knowledge, donating $100 million to a wide range of schools. He plans to donate a total of $2 billion more. Mann has chosen to be a conscious contributor to the evolution of others as part of his own evolution. His leadership is all about a relay—passing on possibility and impact to the generations that follow.[3]

Alfred Mann himself would remind us that many people have been affected by the impact of their own achievements and, in response to the possibilities unleashed, have consciously chosen to contribute to evolution in the lives of others—and of the world at large. Who would decline to follow in their footsteps?

We do, all the time. Too often, the image of a leader like Mann is not inspiring to others; instead, it's daunting. It becomes a reason to dismiss our own call to lead, because we make the mistake of comparison. We can't imagine influencing what is evolving around us to the extent Mann has, so we find another excuse to avoid the need for personal mastery. To break through this false assumption, we must follow the excuse back to its source. It's rooted in the idea that some things cannot change—including ourselves. If we want to lead, we have to break out of the limitations we impose on ourselves. We must pick our heroes and draw on their inspiration.

Alfred Mann is a hero to me because he reminds me that we can make significant contributions to the lives around us by making small changes in ourselves and that the impact of our contributions will create opportunities we never imagined to have even greater impact.

You can count on it.

Welcoming Change

Something else we can count on when we're part of a transformation is that we will feel fear. Fear is a natural response to letting go of familiar things and trying new ones. The best change is the kind that surprises us with its extent and leads us to unimagined achievements.

Leadership requires us to embrace change, transformation and evolution; but the accompanying upheaval and instability, and the unknown potential effects can be frightening. Fear is just a feeling. The question is not how to stop feeling fear; it's how to keep fear from affecting our conscious choices for positive change.

We're not wired for change. In fact, some studies suggest that when a person is forced to change a fundamental belief, his or her brain can undergo the same physiological reactions as the brain of someone who is undergoing torture. Thus, at a certain point, excitement about change is physiologically the same as fear.

And yet, we thrive on change, and we can choose to welcome it. Without change, nothing would ever grow or blossom. We couldn't move forward to become the people we want to be. Change is crucial for growth, advancement and survival. Living in a state of consciousness and vigilance enables us to be actors in our evolution—not victims of unknown forces. Change is ever upon us, and the choice is ours over and over. The toughest thing to change is our mind.

Think about the year you were born and list three things that have come into existence since that year. Say you were born in 1963. Anyone who was an adult at that time can remember life without personal computers, cell phones, and automobile air bags. But if you were born in 1963, you may find it difficult to imagine life without them. This is just one illustration of how our culture, our communities, and we as individuals are evolving every day.

We live in an era marked by an unprecedented abundance of capital and an exponential explosion of ideas. A new century is upon us. More than ever, with the advances around us, leaders are needed to create community and to galvanize the power of community. Leaders are needed to embrace the future, using our collective abilities to unleash individual achievement and challenge complacency.

If you are an executive in a leadership role, it is assumed that you keep up with the advances in your field. Much less is said about making a similar study of your own knowledge, abilities, commitment, habits and interests. Yet, until you are in touch with yourself, you cannot ask others to become conscious of their potential to contribute to an evolving workplace, community or world. The challenge is to continue advancing in consciousness of all your surroundings, not just the technical ones you need to stay competent in your field.

You don't get a certificate for personal mastery. No one gives you a grade, except maybe you yourself. But personal mastery is the differentiating variable in determining the success of organizational transformation. For success, personal mastery must become a way of life.

CHAPTER FOUR

Diving Deep

A Journey from Intention to Legacy

Leaders agree that it's lonely at the top. The isolation can be disorienting, and the choices we make in dealing with it can be painful and drain us of energy. We can even become less effective. On the other hand, the isolation at the top can create a rich, solitary space for private reflection, where leaders can cultivate increasing levels of consciousness and self-honesty. It is here that leaders in motion reach into the depths of themselves to find resource, vision and clarity. Here they ground their sense of commitment and recharge themselves for high-energy interactions with others. When we choose wisely how to use the isolation of leadership, we make it an opportunity for evolution, and it becomes central to our ability to build bonds, develop networks, and inspire others to new commitments.

Isolation is, at its best, a place of dispassion. It enables us to be detached from the dynamic of people that can be so energizing—and so demanding, even draining. For some, it allows time for rejuvenation and reflection. Our choices will depend on whether we benefit from solitude or feel lonely in isolation. We are free to choose whether isolation is a positive or negative force in our leadership.

To maintain the energy we need to lead consciously and to remain honest about what surrounds us, we have to know who we are. We must take stock even as our organization and environment are evolving. For that, we begin in solitude. We step outside our environment, our organization and even most of our relationships. Without distraction or influences that may be guided by hidden agendas, we reflect in safety, honestly. We expand our conscious awareness of all the factors in our experience. Before we lead a group further into change, we take stock of the forces that must be mastered. The first force to master is ourselves.

As a role model for contemporary entrepreneurs and visionaries, Bill Gates took time away from work annually, not just to recharge his batteries but also to create enough distance from his business that he could see the challenges more clearly. He sought solitude, and in solitude he found wisdom. It may sound like an epic myth, but a surprising percentage of leaders take time apart from their daily routines to seek solitude, where they can find new ideas and fresh starts. The leadership impulse for retreat has many roots but a common impact. Abraham Lincoln and his family often took refuge in a cottage on one of the highest hills in Washington, D.C., where he could gaze down through the swampy heat to the Capitol, which was under construction. Some historians have said that it was here, among the cool breezes from the Chesapeake Bay and far from his Cabinet, that Lincoln conceived the first draft of the Emancipation Proclamation.[4] Creating a space apart is not just a geographic exercise but a psychological one as well. Writing about taking up painting in midlife, Winston Churchill described how—in a nation that had been shattered by war—leisure and art provided a refuge and time to regenerate.[5]

Life, business and the people around us change constantly. In fact, it's said that the only constant is change. Without a space we can withdraw to, we cannot regroup, grow and expand. We're at risk of falling into reaction mode, and our choices may cease to be conscious ones.

Intention

The only way to make good choices is to clearly understand what you want. If you have no idea what you want, you can't make choices. If you can't see a destination, you can't begin to imagine the direction in which you must evolve. Progress relies on what you intend to achieve and where you intend to go, and on your very intention to succeed. As Ben Stein, the economist and famous author, says, "The indispensable first step to getting the things you want out of life is this: Decide what you want."[6]

In organizations, we set goals. For some personal improvement programs, we set goals, too. Intention is not to be confused with goals. Intention helps us achieve our goals despite obstacles. It provides the willpower to find the way.

Transformation is guided by intention. Ideally, the guiding intention is cast by the leader like the beam from a lighthouse. Knowing what you really want will help you articulate your intention—first to yourself and then to others. Being conscious of your real intention is crucial. Do you really believe in the goals you've set, or is some part of you holding back? Are you being authentic or false? Only when you make conscious choices to embrace change and a new direction can you lead people toward a better future. Along the way, monitoring your intention is a way of checking how you're progressing.

You cannot maintain a positive direction if your intention is not clear. You cannot give good directions unless you are clear about your intention. Your choices cannot satisfy you unless you understand what you want. In the process that follows, you will consciously contribute to how you evolve, so you must clarify your intention.

Great leaders have clear intention. They encourage the people around them to clarify their intention, too. Any community, including the workplace, involves shared goals. Because we share common goals, everything we do is interconnected. As we all contribute to the goals, our choices are woven together.

Many people seem to think that intention will clarify as circumstances improve, but they're seeing things in reverse. Intention can become clarified at any time, and the sooner the better. Shared goals need unified intention. Without unified intention, the end result will disappoint many contributors, and people can become atomized and frustrated. If we share a goal and unify our intention, we become of one will. We change together, move forward together. We support ongoing transformation by supporting each other. Sound farfetched? Remember some timeless wisdom: Where there's a will, there's a way.

Will is intention. Clarify your intention and you'll release your willpower. Where do you start when you want to clarify your intention? Start with what matters to you. Ask yourself if what matters to you is transformation and growth.

Consider the dramatic moments in life that spur people to act with such total commitment that they refuse to fail, regardless of the obstacles. In those moments, intention is unleashed. Imagine receiving a phone call at work in which you learn that your child or another close family member is gravely ill and needs you immediately. Would you allow any barrier to hold you back? What if, by leaving, you'll miss a critical deadline? What if your boss threatens to fire you if you go? What if your business partner threatens to sue you? What if your car doesn't start?

When clients consider these scenarios, the response is consistently one of determination. People are certain they would do whatever it takes to reach their loved one. When asked how their colleagues would act, people say they would do the same. This is an example of clear intention. It's an illustration of the decisiveness and power that clear intention can release.

Success requires that we develop clear intention if we want to be decisive and achieve results. If we want to contribute to the evolution of our own lives and the lives and work of others, we need clear intention.

Unfortunately, the alternative is common. Constrained by our assumptions about what's possible, we can perceive ourselves as victims of circumstance. This is an example of grave dishonesty with ourselves. It's a human tendency to blame external factors for bad outcomes. We point to impersonal mechanisms as if their influence overrides our own power. But as leaders, when we hear ourselves blaming outside forces for inferior results, we can recognize a warning flare, a signal that it's time to examine how the results demonstrate an intention other than the one we voice. Success requires clear intention to reach the results we say we want.

Here's where the process of personal mastery can be demanding. Most of us do not have truth-tellers who are so close they can call us on our lack of honesty. And even if we do, we can't be sure that they'll always have enough insight to see what's going on and challenge us.

So the responsibility for consciousness remains solely our own, especially if we choose to lead. When we hear ourselves blaming external forces, we must turn to a growing ability to be conscious without hesitation. It is our best shield against the easy out of blaming others and perpetuating a cycle of failure.

Imagine that you've declared to the world your intention to arrive at your office on time. The following Monday morning, you're 10 minutes late. What's your excuse? A good 10-minute reason is that traffic was heavy or the batteries in your alarm clock died. These are factors you can't control, right? So being late is not your fault, right? Now let's raise the bar. Imagine that you're four hours late for work. You need a four-hour reason to explain why the results you demonstrate do not match the intention you announced. Maybe you had a flat tire, or a plumbing leak. What if you don't show up for a week? You need a whopper of reason to explain your results now!

Think about this another way: What would happen if you were guaranteed to receive a million dollars in cash for showing up on time at work Monday morning? What would you do to make sure you weren't late? You might leave home at 3:00 a.m., park in front of your office, and sit in your car until the doors open. Or you might choose to camp overnight on the front steps of your office building. Or, as an extreme measure of caution, you might handcuff yourself to your desk and refuse to leave the building on Friday. But you would intend to be there on Monday morning, and you would actually be there on Monday morning, on time.

The point is simple: When you're clear about your real intention, when you know what you want, you'll find a way. Where there's a will, there's clear intention, and so there's a way. Without intention, there would be no will to find a way.

Imagining

But your intention can't be clear if you can't say what you want. Actually, few of us really know what we want, and fewer still know how to talk about what we want. Most of us do not dare to imagine big enough to match our true potential. Don't forget what Ben Stein said about deciding what you want.

Intention does not emerge out of nowhere. We use reason and imagination to get to it. Reason can help us identify our intention and provide a reality test. But reason also sometimes holds us back. We must be willing to imagine our way ahead. We must consciously choose to imagine. We need to be able to dream, and dream big.

When we imagine what it would look like to be our best, do great things, and have meaningful success, we take personal mastery to higher levels. Our reason is challenged to move beyond the hidden assumptions that might be holding us back. Our imaginations are released to become integral parts of our transformation. Our dreams have a place, and our solitude finds a purpose. The full range of our selves is starting to be integrated in a new, transformative way.

As we forge ahead into ever clearer and braver intention, we burn through our false self-images—the pictures of ourselves that limit us. One far too common self-image is that of victim. If we view ourselves as victims of circumstance, we will find ourselves more and more resigned. Accepting difficult situations is a sign of maturity if we see them as starting points and are ready to evolve from there; but it's quite another thing to be resigned to the notion that there's nothing better than what we can see in the moment and to believe we're at some kind of end point. Acceptance leaves room for us to imagine something different without becoming disheartened. Resignation, on the other hand, means we have to some degree been vanquished by the limits we put on ourselves. It leaves little room to imagine—or to have meaningful success.

To release the creative energy within ourselves—and within those around us—we must reach outside our assumptions and beliefs. If we've resigned ourselves to certain problems, we'll feel trapped and will be unable to imagine new vistas.

Another example of how we constrain our ability to imagine is the way we talk about what we want. Most people are quite willing to say what they don't want. It's easier to say "I don't want chicken for dinner" than to say you want a specific mix of meat and potatoes—or that you've decided to be a vegetarian. That kind of positive assertion requires effort and a certain level of conscious awareness. To be consciously aware is a choice. It's part of the personal mastery leaders must seek. If we want to be able to make positive assertions about our intentions, we have to start learning how to do so.

Even in the most obvious areas, we can see room for growth. If you offer people the choice of being bored or not, most quickly choose not to be bored. But not everyone has a clear idea about what it takes to avoid boredom. In fact, boredom is often just a lack of knowledge about an alternative action. You're the only person who knows how you can avoid being bored, but do you have a clear idea of what you need to stay busy and engaged? Have you made the conscious choice to know yourself and to create a clear intention not to be bored?

The contradiction between what we say we want and what we actually do is a signal we can learn to read: It signals a lack of clear intention. Watch for the contradiction. There you'll find the insight you need.

Most of us want to be healthy. Certainly hardly anyone would admit to wanting to be ill. But many of us don't make choices for a healthy life. We've all heard about people who lead unhealthy lives for years and then have a eureka moment, a wake-up call, and suddenly find the motivation to do whatever it takes to turn their lives around. The catalyst could be a health crisis or seeing a reflection in the mirror with new eyes; somehow intention is clarified and resignation to old habits disappears. What has long seemed impossible can be achieved, because clear intention activates and energizes us. Intention is sparked by imagining and, in turn, unleashes possibilities. Personal evolution without clarified intention will be stalled. As we imagine fresh, brave, new intention, our transformation progresses and creates more and more possibilities.

The clearer your intention, the farther you will go—into places and at levels that you've not even dreamed about before. Be sure to take your imagination with you!

Unimaginable Possibilities

You've spent some time dreaming big. You've been brave enough to name your intention, challenging your sense of reason to stretch beyond its former self. Even so, you cannot imagine all the possibilities that lie before you. It's important to be flexible, so you're ready for the unimagined possibilities for which your transformation is the catalyst.

Seeking to discover unimagined possibilities is the work of leaders. When we can begin to imagine fresh, new possibilities, we have a signal that our personal freedom is being unleashed. A leader is often defined as the person who unleashes the imaginations of those who surround him to achieve great ends. But the first step for each of us is to persist in our own process of personal mastery.

Once we imagine the most courageous intention, we must break through what inhibits our imaginations. The only way to do this is to let intention guide us—in fact, to let it drive us. Intention can be clear but not easily articulated. Sometimes our intention stretches to places before we can even imagine them, yet we are clear because we are motivated. At times, we sense possibility before we can define it. That's no reason not to let it inspire us about ourselves or about the future.

I discovered that clear intention could lead me well beyond anything I could imagine when I was still very young, growing up in eastern Tennessee. I was the child of tobacco farmers, and we did not have a telephone until I was 12. There was little reason to go to the store, because we raised most of the food we ate. I didn't go to a restaurant until I was 15. So the images of the world at large barely reached me. It was hard to imagine that world, let alone what my future might be if I ventured into it. I seemed to have little that would help clarify my intention. And yet, at the age of 14, I found clear intention that ultimately led me to meaningful success 25 years later.

Our Chevy Impala was a focal point for the family. My father had bought it for $95 and painted it himself. Every weekend (during the summer, every weekday), we drove 30 minutes to the farm owned by my mother's family, There we kids joined in for 10-hour days, side by side with my parents and the rest of the family, working in the tobacco fields and vegetable gardens, and helping take care of the chickens, pigs and cows. What defines that time for me are memories of dragging myself out of bed to get a bite of breakfast before piling into the car, and longing for a single day of sleep on weekends during the school year or a few days off during the lazy, hot summers. I remember being dirty and sticky from tending tobacco plants for hours in the unrelenting sun. My intention started as a negative. I knew what I didn't want. I didn't want to be tied to farm work for the rest of my life.

Lacking any real idea of my options in the world beyond eastern Tennessee, you might think it would be impossible to define a positive idea of what I wanted, that I'd be stuck defining myself in negative terms. How could I imagine without knowing? But I did. In that rural corner of the world, I was able to find images of positive ways to define my intention, even if I couldn't imagine where it would lead me.

One of my most enduring memories is the image of Dad's hands, which were sometimes torn and bleeding from working his factory job with a furniture manufacturer. The wood on the production line often splintered and cut the workers' hands. But he seemed unaware of the discomfort, as he hoed the endless weeds or lifted the heavy farm equipment. He worked without respite. I remember lifting my eyes up from the task at hand and glancing over the rows at him. When I did, I would also see the undeniable beauty all around us. The splendor of the setting connected me with him, and with my mother and her extended family, as we worked in our little spheres, apart from each other in the field we were sharing. Those moments took my breath away, even when I was very young. I can remember how connected I felt to the earth and to the people I loved.

Around us were 260 acres of dense woods, rolling green pastures, and meticulously plowed fields. When we had breaks from work, we explored the expanse of the farm, finding quiet places to play, lounging in the fields, staring for long stretches of time up at cotton-ball clouds tumbling across the endless blue sky. I felt gentle country breezes cooling my hot brow and cheeks. Fresh from hard work, I breathed the crisp, clean air. My daydreams began to wander into my future. Some days I wondered how I could ever be more, do more, see more, have more. But other days, in that setting, I felt as though nothing could hold me back.

Whenever my imagination broke out beyond what I knew, my intention was being clarified. When it was time to head back after a weekend on the farm, I watched my father's hands on the steering wheel as he drove his tired family home. He had clear intention to provide for us. In his example, I was finding a path toward success that neither of us envisioned at the time.

My family was focused on hard work. From a young age I was not restrained from contributing like an adult, so my idea about what I was capable of was not nearly as narrow as that of most kids my age. I was free to believe whatever I could imagine. My intention slowly found its articulation: to become my most bold, beautiful, brilliant and benevolent self. I began to repeat this idea to myself over and over. I had found a clear intention. I was on my way.

The challenge is to develop our consciousness and self-awareness to the point that we know what we want. We start by clarifying our intention, but that's just the beginning. Leaders don't just have clear intention but also an overall sense of clarity that informs every decision. Clarity ensures that leaders don't get bogged down in indecision. Clarity keeps leaders in motion.

Intention has some basic building blocks. In life and in work, if we know the things we want, we can begin to focus our intention. But few people can state what they want. At best, they define themselves by negatives, by what they don't want or what they're not likely to do. We need to press beyond this limiting point of view until we can make positive assertions about what we want. Then we can have clearer ideas about our intention.

Start with today. What do you really want? Challenge yourself with this question. Your energy is limited. Your life is limited. Knowing this, what do you want from investing your life's energy at this moment, for this day?

An exercise like this one can help you get clear on what you want. You may need to take a day or two off to reflect quietly on your own. A smart step is to turn to a mentor or trusted colleague for feedback on your ideas. You can find some wonderful mentors in books, but don't think you have to muddle your way through, thinking and reading in isolation. There are people in your life right now who would be happy to act as a sounding board outside your work setting, and they can challenge your habits and false assumptions better than you can. You might even choose to work with the TSI tools or one of our teams in a workshop.

What matters is that you pull yourself away from the assumptions that prevail in your daily life. Only then can you break out of what is holding you back and eventually blaze a trail for those around you and for your organization.

What do you want? Think of a three-legged stool. You must know what you want for yourself, for your relationships, and for your organization if you are to emerge as a leader. These are the three legs of the stool. The stool will falter with instability if you focus too much on one or forget about another. Balance is a crucial part of clarifying intention. Ideally, you'll be inspired to want many things in all three areas, but only by knowing what you want can you clarify your intention and order your priorities.

Great leaders are characterized by their clarity, commitment and energy. In his best-selling book *Good to Great: Why Some Companies Make the Leap .. and Others Don't,* Jim Collins asserts that great leaders have something he calls "professional will" or "professional intention." Collins says that only a leader who exhibits clear professional intention can create superb results and be a catalyst for transformation. This is the kind of executive who shows unwavering resolve to do whatever must be done to produce the best long-term results, no matter how difficult. Collins says that professional intention leads an executive to look in the mirror, not out the window, when results are poor, and never to blame other people, external mechanisms or bad luck.

Thus, Collins believes that leadership begins with personal mastery, and clear intention begins quite close to home. With clear intention—the clarity characteristic of authentic leadership—leaders remain vigilant, constantly conscious of how results do or do not demonstrate their stated intention. Intention remains clear, and expectations that are constantly measured against intentions produce the desired results.

Unity

A group of people with clear intention can be a powerful force when they unify their focus and potential. But unless each person has clear intention, that is impossible to do. If each person has clear intention, a leader can be a pivotal focal point for interconnectedness. The leader can integrate intention by communicating a vision that unites and channels collective energy.

David Wright, chief operating officer for Capital One (Europe), was the director of data center services when he talked with me about uniting people's energy using easy tools—like roundtables to promote a balanced discussion or a tennis ball marked with a question mark and thrown to different people—to energize the dynamic of the group. He said, "Uniting people's energy is an ongoing process. It's how you work with people. It's important to have cross-functional teams form and reform on an ongoing basis."

When a leader is willing to promote unity within a group, a power is tapped to achieve truly great ends that no one could achieve alone. Wright described it this way: "Power is the combined ability to see a desired future, and to state and communicate it in a way that compels people to action." Another way of looking at it is that leaders start from a place of solitude and create connectedness and achievement. Unity permits the relay of intention, values, energy and success among members of the group.

One exceptional leader tells how his belief in the impact of clear intention and the power of unified intention came into focus in a remarkable adventure. Dr. Richard G. Stieglitz is the founder of RGS Associates, author of *Taming the Dragons of Change:10 Tips for Achieving Happiness and Success When Everything Around You is Changing*, and a valued colleague. A few years ago, Dick participated in a series of self-awareness classes to enhance his leadership abilities. One session took place over a weekend. At 9:00 p.m. on Saturday, after a full day of class work, the 24-person group received its assignment for Sunday. The assignment was to feed 90 homeless people at 9:00 the following morning. The class had 12 hours and zero resources. They were prohibited from using any personal resources, such as cash or credit cards. The assignment was to go out and create results from nothing. The instructors said good night and left.

The general response was "How do we do something like this?" No one in the class had any experience preparing a meal event, especially from scratch and with no resources. Everyone was tired from the full day of classes. They were in a strange city and didn't know anybody. Finally, someone thought to ask, "If we did create a breakfast, what would we need?" The group determined that, first, they would need dishes, silverware, and pots and pans. Then they would need food: bacon, eggs, bread, fruit, milk and butter. Third, they would need decorations. They divided themselves into three teams, eight to a team. None of the teams really knew where to start, but at least they could clarify their intention. Dick was on the food team; their goal was to find bacon and eggs and bread for 90 people without any resources.

Fortunately, they were in a city where many stores stay open all night. First, Dick's team went to bakeries. One bakery gave them 12 pies. Then they went to supermarkets. Most turned them away, and some were very rude. However, a few gave them good food. They scoured the streets until, by 2:00 a.m., they had collected what they needed. They were amazed. They had acquired all the food they needed in just a few hours. They had no idea how the other two teams were faring. They decided to get some sleep and have faith that the other groups would muster the same energy and creativity and produce the same kind of results.

The next morning, Dick's group showed up at the breakfast location early. By 10:00 a.m., the 24 class members had fed 90 people, and they had a blast doing it. The next problem was figuring out where to donate the excess food and the balloons and streamers. The group had fed 90 people using nothing but intention and teamwork. United intention will create great results!

Intention is the foundation for teamwork and collective success. But it begins with each person becoming clear about what he or she really wants. United intention among a group of committed people can be boosted by other factors, such as integrity, consciousness and vision. But it is born in a process of personal mastery, when we look fearlessly within. As our intention gains in clarity, we are drawn toward others—and our work in personal mastery begins to venture outward from a place of solitary reflection.

Vision

Intention is very closely related to vision, and when intention among the contributors moving forward together toward a goal is unified, a vision can become reality. Intention drives a leader and contributors to return to the daily challenge and forge ahead, but in doing so they feed off a shared vision of what might be. Vision and visionaries inspire people and groups, stoke their energy, and unify them.

The idea of a leader mastering him- or herself is a visionary one that we at TSI promote because we've seen the concrete results when the vision becomes reality. Guided by the vision of leadership that is unwilling to rest on yesterdays' laurels, our leaders are willing to connect their own conscious evolution to that of the organization. They are willing to be known and to commit to really knowing the people, work and marketplace that comprise their world.

The word *vision* is rooted in words that mean both "sight" and "knowing." In ancient Greek, the root word *veda* meant "to know." The Anglo-Saxon and Old French versions of the word in the 13th century equated seeing with knowing, even with revelation. Latin emphasized the idea of seeing and vision as one of the senses, implying that what is seen is known. We see what we know. We see clearly what we know clearly. Clarified intention lies at the core of a leader's vision.

The idea of vision is very close to the idea of intention. To see is to know. Vision is what we see, or the dream we visualize. Intention is the way we know the vision, the dream, and our own commitments and capacities. Vision clarifies intention.[7]

Legacy

Unity leads to legacy. A leader offers clarity, commitment and energy to the group and receives the same in return from the group. Transformation is under way, the leader is in motion, and a forceful group of interconnected people are creating a long-term impact. Legacy is impact over the long haul.

Leaders leave a legacy that defines them, but the organizations they led have also defined them. So legacy, in the best circumstances, is circular, reflecting the organization in the leader and the leader in the organization. Legacies often are stories of the circularity of commitment and caring.

One of the most wonderful opportunities my work offers is that I regularly interact with leaders. In one instance, I heard the story of how the vision and commitment of two leaders resulted in a legacy where nothing had been. It is a story of something coming from, quite literally, nothing. The lasting success that has touched generations came from the courses of action taken by two different leaders at two unexpected junctures. In the case of the leader who inherited the work of the first to finish (or to abandon, as she chose), it is also the story of how we may inherit opportunities, but we must still bring our full potential as leaders to bear. This is what happened to Eileen McCaffrey, executive director of the Orphan Foundation of America; she inherited a legacy and passed one on.

Eileen's foster brother, the Reverend Joseph Rivers, was an amazing man. He had grown up in foster care and ultimately devoted his life to battling against the obstacles that held most foster care children back. As he struggled to emerge from the foster care system into the life of a successful adult, he found no real support for making this difficult transition. He was able to attend college only by working his way through. When he arrived in Washington, D.C., after college, he talked to Eileen all the time about how he wanted to use his experience and ideas to help others like himself. Joseph drew on his own difficulties and pain to imagine ways to help other foster children follow in his footsteps.

Joseph established the Orphan Foundation of America (OFA) in 1981. At that time, professionals and policymakers were not talking about how to help children "age out" of the system. Joseph was forging a path where no one else had thought to go. With relentless effort, he galvanized volunteers, becoming known in Washington as someone who was dedicated to helping others "age out" of the system, and his dedication to other orphans meant he would not take no for an answer. His passion was fueled by his intention that other kids must be spared the obstacles he had faced. Sometimes his single-minded focus seemed to be tinged with an anger people didn't understand, but then, they hadn't faced the struggle Joseph had during his youth. He earned respect over the years from many people who otherwise had not been focusing on the plight of orphans as they grew up.

Then, in 1986, after keeping the organization going by the sheer force of his will for five years, Joseph received a donation of $10,000. He used it to give $2,500 scholarships to four local foster care students who hoped to attend college.

Five years later, just as the foundation was beginning to stabilize, Joseph Rivers died. What was left was Joseph's vision and his unwavering determination not to chase funding but to remain focused on a core group of foster kids whose individual success was the shared goal of the group. That approach meant, however, that Joseph left very little money to sustain his work. His vision seemed to have come to an end. He had died too young.

After the funeral, Eileen found herself sorting through her brother's files. In them, she discovered applications for the few scholarships he had offered. They revealed fervor and talent and hope among the young people. They documented heroic success stories. As she read these stories, Eileen became aware of how everyone, including professionals in the system, had little hope to offer foster children who were trying to move into adult lives. It was impossible not to see how much communities could offer if only someone would keep working to tap the goodwill. Eileen could see no dollars set aside to help these kids transition—no money or programs in agency budgets and no money in the foundation's budget either. She couldn't walk away.

It was a decisive moment. The first step was small compared with what the Orphan Foundation of America does now: The board created a national scholarship fund in Joseph's name and raised $30,000 in the first year. As applications poured in, Eileen read them, weeping to think that these kids, with so much resilience and potential, might not have a chance to thrive. She started to understand Joseph's anger, because many people still assumed that most of these kids would never amount to much. Eileen realized that Joseph's vision had affected her, and she was moved to pick up the torch. She had never expected to lead a national foundation or cause, but she stepped into the role.

Early on, Eileen had the vision of bringing foster kids to Washington to learn, grow and meet with their congressional representatives. Her work gave them a voice, but they communicated their issues not just through words. The remarkable spirit and potential of these young people were obvious to all who met them. In his vision, Joseph saw what no one else could see—the potential of these children waiting to be tapped. Eileen's work focused a spotlight on this vision. Views of foster children started to change.

Soon the board decided to translate the concept into a national program. Now, for the 25,000 kids aging out of foster care each year, there are many options. Scholarships are granted. Mentor and intern programs offer experience and growth to many young people. Among the foundation's programs is the Red Scarf Program, in which a red scarf is presented to foster children as they head off to college. Eileen and the foundation grew into their role of advancing Joseph's vision of caring for children with the utmost integrity. This is how many of us come into our leadership roles: unexpectedly.

Eileen imparts the idea of integrity in many ways—to the children, volunteers, alums and donors. OFA receives the highest score possible for fundraising efficiency from one of the nation's leading charity evaluators. The importance of those who benefit from its services permeates the foundation. Eileen's leadership embodies service—she is not only the president of OFA but also a mentor to many children in the program. In her many interactions with the children, she reminds them that she is only the temporary caretaker of the foundation; it is their organization. Her values of education, belonging and opportunity color every program the foundation promotes. Through these programs, Eileen shows the children that they are more than "foster kids," and she encourages them to give back— not necessarily through OFA but to those in need of help. She imparts vision and values more in deed than in word. Joseph's legacy will continue beyond Eileen and beyond OFA, in the promising futures of these new leaders. This is leadership potential few believed in when Joseph founded OFA in 1981.

As I listened to Eileen's story, I heard the clarity, commitment and energy of a leader whose abilities have been unleashed by opportunity. She said, "You have to be really centered and really clear on what your values are, and not get sidetracked along the way by money or negative influences. It's easy in our society to spin out of control. The clarity of staying true to self is critical, and you must understand that everyone is smarter than you."

Joseph's intention was clear, and his work was single-minded. His integrity was revealed in his core value of focusing on the kids and not on the money or other distractions of running a nonprofit. He trained his consciousness on the foster children, and Eileen has done the same. What they both wanted was what was right for the kids. Their intentions were unified. They let nothing stand in their way, but they were not so driven that they forced solutions when evolution, not a fast fix, was needed.

For Eileen, legacy has been part of her work every day since her passion for this cause was ignited. How do we start today to leave a legacy now, instead of waiting until the end of our career or the end of our life? Eileen defines legacy as something bigger and better than simply profit or donations. She said, "Passion and zest are what seem to be missing for some people. When you're hunkered down and protecting what's yours, you don't feel so good. When you're giving, you feel great!"

Regardless of whether your leadership role is in a nonprofit organization, a government agency or a commercial venture, contributing to the growth of others is a big part of what you do. Embodying values and vision is what you do. Only through personal mastery can you open yourself up enough to be able to do this.

Continuity

Intention needs continuity to flourish. Unity is a kind of continuity, and legacy is—by its very nature—all about continuity. Transformation itself draws out a continuity unique to each setting. Diving deep into ourselves, we can find our own source of energy, which provides continuity despite the changes around us.

Bobby Ukrop, president and CEO of Ukrop's Super Markets in Richmond, Virginia, believes that a central factor in his successful grocery retail business is continuity of leadership and how that has earned the trust of customers, suppliers and associates. During a session we had a few years ago, Bobby said, "We have teenagers whose first job is with Ukrop's, and those who choose us as a career, and we are the last-paying job for the many part-time senior citizens. We want to be a positive influence and serve as good role models."

Ukrop's is a business that has blazed trails through constant transformation. A family business founded in 1937, Ukrop's only had one store until 1963, when Bobby's brother Jim created a multi-store operation. Based on the growth of the number of stores (18 by 1987 and approximately 2,000 associates), the brothers formalized a Mission Statement fifty years after the business began.

With its commitment to change and its steady leadership, Ukrop's began to reject the typical model for traditional supermarket companies, which established clear rules that restrict the latitude of their managers in making decisions. Bobby explained that Ukrop's evolved out of that model in the 1970s when the family decided it was time to become even more customer-driven and decentralized. The goal was to empower the entire staff to serve people better. Again, in 1993, Ukrop's leadership took its company through another period when how it defined leadership changed even more. Leadership became something expected of each associate. "We need," Bobby explained of the evolving culture, "associates who can *think* more, using good judgment and values to make decisions. We have empowered our associates to become even more customer-oriented." To show its associates the importance of their role in its service model, the family gives 20 percent of pre-tax profits back to associates every quarter, and the family does not participate in that program. Meanwhile, top management is exploring other opportunities for rewards for long-term thinking and smart actions.

Ukrop's value of continuity is not reflected only in the full engagement of family members. Bobby believes that leaders need to be visible and be good role models, but he expects the same of all associates. When I last met with him, Ukrop's was celebrating 80 delicatessen associates who had begun their careers more than 15 years earlier. Soon after that, Ukrop's was to celebrate more than 50 octogenarian employees, and there were 170 associates between the ages of 70 and 79. At Ukrop's, associates are leaders, too, empowered to make good decisions in their service of others and valued for doing so. This culture of transformation inspires loyalty that retains associates and provides continuity in every customer interaction.

CHAPTER FIVE

Challenging Ourselves

Freedom on the Other Side of the Jump

Self-challenge is an important part of self-mastery. There can be no real clarity, commitment or energy without it. Leaders stagnate without it. Transformation becomes an exercise in directives and micromanagement without the willingness of all contributors to an organizational goal to challenge first themselves and then others. This is especially true for leaders. They must be in the habit of challenging what they know, feel, assume and achieve if they expect the organization to continue to transform and thrive.

Personal mastery is an evolutionary process beginning at our core, where the isolation of leadership is productive solitude full of reflection and honesty. There we become more and more conscious of ourselves as leaders—and as individuals. This discovery process often unleashes energy and enthusiasm, which we can bring with us to lead the group dynamic to higher levels of energy and creativity. Sometimes, however, our enthusiasm leads us to challenge others prematurely. In the process, we can create barriers instead of creating better connections. Before we, as leaders, can effectively challenge others to new ways of acting, we must first challenge ourselves. We must learn the art of self-challenge.

When we challenge ourselves, we draw truths from deep within— not about others but about ourselves. Challenging ourselves is just another level of self-awareness. It drives us to higher levels of being honest with ourselves. It demands that we make conscious choices about how we behave, how we think, and how we interact with others. Our commitment to leadership takes a great leap forward.

People are drawn to leaders who are self-aware, and those leaders have a confidence that warrants the trust others place in them. As leaders enter into relationships with others, both inside and outside the organization, their self-awareness helps them identity the truly rewarding and positive connections, and influence less constructive connections to improve their ability to contribute to the goals. Once we understand the connections we develop with others, we can begin to share our vision with them and use our own intention to inspire success.

But before these connections with others can be fruitful, we must spend time challenging ourselves to admit and change habits that otherwise will prove counterproductive to the synergistic connections we seek. Self-challenge is cyclical. Each time we assess our habits, we advance to a higher level of personal integrity because, grounded anew in our core values, we can refine our ideas and attitudes about success, learning and winning.

The best news about this sometimes difficult process is that our mistakes can be contributors to our success. It's even possible to be grateful for failures. Our whole approach to learning and growth changes, often quite radically. We can let go of the habit of beating ourselves up and appreciate life's ups and downs. Self-challenge is an opportunity to make peace with our own lives. With that sense of calm, we can change our minds or our approaches without much upheaval. We are consciously choosing new reactions. Often, these changes do not create discomfort; rather, they bring peace of mind. The connections we foster become more flexible and open, more honest and productive. We have less to prove to others, because we've already challenged ourselves to respond in new ways.

Self-challenge is about adjusting our minds; that is, it's about choosing the attitudes we will have. We start to see how much power attitudes have over our own lives and the lives around us. The more positive the new attitude is, the more positive our reactions based on it can be. Positive outcomes increase. This is a recipe for personal serenity that offsets the many demands of leadership and serves as an antidote to the stress experienced by those around us.

It begins with our own reactions. Reacting differently is often a tactical matter, because many bad habits are nothing more than poorly chosen reactions. Chaotic days or schedules are driven by old habits; a leader can regain order and calm by developing new habits. Inefficient patterns can become more efficient. Haste that undermines an ability to listen can become focus and calm. We can reduce our own stress level and, thus, the stress around us. We can see how the energy we bring to the dynamic with those we lead is greatly affected by how we arrive as individuals.

With time and practice, self-challenge turns into a new level of success that is personal but has a broad impact. A new image of our leadership takes root. We become grounded as individuals first and then as increasingly effective leaders. There's no longer a reason to avoid being alone; we are at peace with ourselves and find in solitude much insight and energy to tap for lives that are often very social and group-oriented. We begin to naturally share our confidence, peace and purpose with others.

Cautionary Note

Keeping leaders in motion does have some risk. While we encourage leaders to challenge themselves consciously and constantly, this recommendation needs clarification.

Self-challenge as a habit looks freely at the good and the bad, the wonderful and the less-than-wonderful, the successes and the failures. It seeks to be nonjudgmental, because judgment interferes with clarity. But when people assess themselves, they often focus on the negative. They confuse willingness to be honest with an impulse for self-criticism.

Leaders tend to be high achievers. It is not uncommon for them to be driven—and pretty rough on themselves. So while anyone can benefit from some self-criticism from time to time, your self-assessment will be lopsided if you focus only on the negatives, on mistakes and failures. A leader in motion is most definitely *not* a high-achiever whose self-criticism is in high gear! If you are at risk of being just that, the process of challenging yourself to higher levels will be limited to focusing on things that make you feel bad about yourself and ignoring all the good qualities and talents that can offset your short-comings. In short, self-challenge is not an exercise in self-criticism. It aims for self-knowledge.

Criticism can be very important to leaders. No one can continue advancing to greater levels of effectiveness on the strength of affirmations and popularity. The ability to acknowledge our mistakes can lead us to new learning. Without criticism, our experience counts for little and our daily effectiveness does not advance to match the challenges at hand.

We need to be ready to step into the rich space of solitude and honestly reflect on our attitudes and reactions. We need to be willing to draw more food for thought from others' feedback. But what should be a dispassionate self-examination often becomes self-destructive—an excuse for driving ourselves harder, judging ourselves before anyone else can, and feeding any sense of insecurity we may harbor.

Self-challenge is an opportunity to confront old tapes that play loudly in our heads, insisting that we're less than we really are. We must confront fears about loss and failure on our way to success.

Outside the Comfort Zone

As we evolve, we face the inescapable fact that it is impossible to walk the road of life holding hands with comfort while simultaneously changing. We must be prepared to let go of comfort regularly, choosing transformation over the comfortable status quo. When faced with the chance to step outside our comfort zone, we must exert our will over our habits. That's how we choose consciously to react in new ways. Each time we confront this choice, we must decide all over again whether or not to be a leader. And we must act.

Pushing ourselves to be our best is a crucial commitment for leaders, and it involves continuous change. Change is uncomfortable, even for leaders. Sometimes, in fact, change is even more painful for leaders. The circumstances leading to change can be more isolating, and we can be operating with the false idea that we have no models or mentors.

Every day offers new challenges to our effectiveness that require us to choose whether to improve or to entrench. Every new business opportunity presents us with the invitation to step out into what is not known. To master anything, including ourselves, we have to venture into unknown territory. In retrospect, discovery and growth may be wonderful, but anticipating the first step can be daunting—so much so that it may render us unable to go forward.

A comfort zone is a paradigm of belief. It has developed as we've learned to relate to the world around us. A comfort zone can be crucial. Touching a hot stove with a bare hand, a child quickly learns to believe that doing so in the future will result in another painful burn. This particular comfort zone (hot stoves are dangerous) protects children from injury.

However, comfort zones can hold us back. As evolution tugs us into the unknown, our comfort zones tempt us to reach for what we know. If we choose comfort over growth, we may be opting for the greater risk.

Whatever learning led us into a comfort zone does not remain as constant as the danger of a hot burner. Circumstances change, and what is comfortable—and safe—changes, too. Our comfort zones often are constructed from past circumstances. In our effort to cling to safety, we don't realize that we are becoming less safe by not changing. Thus, our comfort zones, if left unquestioned, limit us and can even harm us.

As leaders, we know that the only way to stay ahead is to seek continuous growth. Growth requires new reactions. Challenging ourselves to react in new ways is the best way to inspire transformation in those around us.

The 300-Foot Precipice

Evolution and transformation are smoothly flowing words, but growth is often not gracious—or even pretty. However, it is consistently essential, often memorable, and sometimes downright comical.

Our trips home from a sweltering weekend or extended summer stay working the family farm in eastern Tennessee were short and hot. As a little girl, I watched my father's calloused hands on the steering wheel of that $95, spray-painted Chevy Impala. We worked as a family with limited means and careful frugality. We could not afford the luxury of a meal at a restaurant. Now, in a single day, I might attend meetings in two or three cities along the mid-Atlantic coast, flying between sessions or driving a new car (painted at the factory) and eating all my meals in restaurants. In retrospect, it seems like a straight trajectory from eastern Tennessee to here, but the process was actually more like finding my way over one 300-foot precipice after another. One precipice in particular was quite literal, and it illustrates how transformation can seem like choosing to tackle a vertical drop on a downhill ski slope without any skis.

When I made the decision to work my way through college, it meant that my parents would be one pair of hands short in the exhausting effort to keep the family afloat. But they and my brothers fully supported my decision, so my intention to succeed was, in part, driven by a desire to honor the sacrifice they had made. The paradigm of my life was hard work, throughout my undergraduate studies at the University of Tennessee and my graduate studies at Virginia Tech. I always worked two or three jobs to pay for my education, and the last couple of years getting my doctorate were fraught with difficulties. When I finally received the degree, my husband Bob took me on a ski trip to celebrate.

The prospect of learning to ski at Lake Tahoe, where people go for some of the best skiing in the country, made me feel more uneasy than thrilled. Skiing was outside my paradigm, outside my comfort zone, and from the moment I arrived, I felt out of my element among so many people skilled at a fast-paced leisure activity. All I could do was—as I had done for years—act as I saw others act and dress as I saw others dress. I was relieved when the instructor on the Bunny slope told us that, with work and over time, we could progress to harder and harder slopes. Work was something I understood. I threw myself into the lesson.

And I learned fast. Fresh off the Double Black Diamond slopes to check on me, Bob was amazed at my progress and offered to take me to a slope one level harder. I sped down the Green slope, exhilarated. The thrill of rushing so freely through the sun and cold was second only to the shock of being outside in nature just for fun, not to work. I felt great surges of energy and confidence. Nothing could stop me. I was ready for anything. I had conquered mountains.

When Bob suggested we try a slope just one level more difficult, it was easy to override the funny feeling I had inside. Riding up on the lift, I noticed that other people's skis were two feet longer than my Bunny slope skis. I hoped that didn't matter. When I started down the slope, however, I immediately felt the new terrain taxing everything in me, and I struggled along a foot at a time. At the bottom of a 300-foot drop-off, Bob pulled to a stop and looked back up at me. I was looking down at him from a dead stop at the top of the precipice, without the momentum of a downhill run to carry me over it. Other skiers whizzed by and yelled at me to make the leap—for my safety and theirs.

I had no frame of reference for how to solve this problem. I simply didn't know what to do. My ability to imagine solutions was paralyzed by my fear. I started to yell furiously at Bob. How could he have led me to this cliff? (He told me later that one skier who passed me yelling on the ledge called out to him, "I feel for you! She's mad!") Bob tried to answer me with hand motions and shouts I couldn't hear. Finally, a skier took pity, stopped, and said, "I think that guy is telling you to take off your skis and climb down the bank."

I was humiliated. A few minutes earlier, I had been in command of the slopes. Now what choice did I have? I took off my skis, slid them down to Bob, and climbed slowly and miserably backwards down the 300-foot drop. Skiers were speeding around me the whole time. When I reached Bob, I stormed that I would never do anything like this again. But then, to my horror, I realized that we weren't at the base of the mountain yet. There were more drop-offs to go. I relied on the adrenaline in my system to put my skis back on and fumble the rest of the way down. Once safely at the base, I said I needed to be alone and strode away from Bob. I sat in the coffee shop, hurt and angry.

It would have been a good time to laugh. Instead, old tapes started to play at full volume. (These are the tapes we try to avoid hearing by avoiding reflecting in quiet and solitude.) My tapes started with recriminations that I took on too dangerous a risk, but soon the tapes settled into a couple old favorites: "Hicks don't belong here. If you have too much fun, something bad will happen." So there I sat, using old tapes to form a new paradigm: Skiing is impossible for someone like me.

Bob and a friend came into the coffee shop. They urged me to get back on the slopes right away. Our friend Jeff handed me a coin. It was engraved with the figure of a skier racing downhill. He said, "Look at this. All you have to remember is to stay calm and keep your center of gravity low." The image broke through my imaginings and let me hear Bob and Jeff. The coin showed the thrill and freedom of the slopes. Suddenly, I could visualize myself on the slopes, with my center of gravity low .. having a blast! I knew what I wanted. I went for it. My fear had not abated, but I was determined to master the slopes. I put my ski boots back on (and shook in them on my way to the lift).

Sure enough, after an hour or so of skiing, I was able to incorporate the feedback, but only after I had visualized myself on the slopes. With encouragement, I'd gotten back up to try again; with effort, I was improving with each run. I was learning a lot. Most of all, I was learning to fall. Was I sore? Absolutely.

Throughout the week, I gained more insight into myself every day and more skill in the sport. My mind was made up. I would live inside the visual image on the coin Jeff had given me. My efforts to ski became more and more effective. By the end of the week, I had advanced superbly. Crawling down the 300-foot precipice had become a life-changing breakthrough and a funny story. From then on, skiing became a process of practicing and using feedback to help me move to new levels of effectiveness—and new and beautiful heights!

Visualization

The image on the coin Jeff handed me was the perfect antidote to the old tapes playing over and over again, and holding me back. It was a focus for my imagination.

The word *vision* is rooted in words that mean both *sight* and *knowing*. *Visualization* is rooted in the idea that vision is reality.

Through visualization, we harness the power of seeing to gain the power of knowing, becoming, achieving.

Visualization is an important aspect of effectiveness. When I was coping with feelings of humiliation and powerlessness after the episode on the 300 foot precipice, I needed to visualize myself skiing, in motion, succeeding by surrendering to a direction (downhill) I had chosen. I needed to visualize a positive outcome to my conscious choice. Only then could I try again.

If I'd recoiled into my comfort zone, I would have resigned myself to never becoming the image on the coin. Before I could give the slopes another try, I had to override the desire to avoid discomfort. I had to be willing to step out of my comfort zone. And this time the step into discomfort was more difficult, because I had already failed. This time the world outside my comfort zone was worse than unknown; it was a scary prospect. I needed the power of visualization.

Visualization can be an antidote to failure. It can be used to override the fears and unhappy images created by our old tapes of self-criticism and self-doubt. Visualizations can become affirmations. By visualizing, you help yourself find a way to achieve your intention. Visualization is conscious choice in action. The means to the end becomes obvious. This is a proven method for finding the best way when you have the will. Where there is intention, there is a way. Where there is visualization, there is already success.

When you dare to imagine that what you want is already your reality, the mindset you foster is not one of recklessness or a way to tempt fate. With visualization you combat self-doubt, find the courage to move outside your comfort zone, and generate the energy and courage to plant a flag on your own personal mountaintop.

All you need is the right mindset, and you can take a step out, succeeding even as you begin.

Walking Around

You can project leadership in everything from how you dress and carry yourself to how you behave. When a leader embodies an image of everything an organization aspires to, she is well on her way to creating a legacy. Like the skier on the coin did for me, leaders can be visual images of where they're directing the evolution of their enterprise. At times, they are visualizations of something greater than themselves. Sometimes leaders embody vision.

Leaders rise to this challenge in many ways. One way is simple: They walk around. When employees see a leader routinely walking around, listening and being available and open, they see a leader in motion. They know that transformation based on the value of everyone's contribution is authentic. Walking around is not just a way for leaders to bond with employees and communicate one-on-one with all levels of a group. It's a way for the leader to communicate by visualization.

Oddly, many leaders postpone walking around and being available to talk to staff. They consider it a luxury and feel as though they don't have time for it. Most leaders agree that walking around can have a powerful impact, but almost as many make excuses or put it off.

Walking around is a way to connect with others, but some leaders have a hard time doing it. They must dive deep into themselves and look at their resistance to such a valuable practice. Walking around is a leadership practice that can be associated with the advanced social skills expected of leaders. It's also a good example of how personal mastery must precede the development of other skills.

When you're pressed to step far out of your comfort zone to do things unique to a leader, you may have a hard time finding support. Perhaps no one else is thinking at that level. Isolation can set in. But you can choose to transform the separation into an opportunity, to discover more about yourself, and to turn to mentors. Mentors may be our contemporaries or towering historical figures whose examples inspire us. When it comes to the art of walking around, Sir Winston Churchill is a good example.

As England's first lord of the admiralty from 1911 to 1915, Churchill visited more ships and naval facilities than any first lord before or since. Between 1911 and the outbreak of World War I in 1914, he visited more than 50 ships, as well as numerous harbor and shipyard sites. This practice was unheard of in military leadership or political life, and it ignored deeply ingrained social sanctions against members of the upper class mixing with those of the lower classes.

But Churchill made it a regular practice to do just that. He listened. He allowed himself to be led. He learned how the Royal Navy operated down to its daily routines. His presence elevated the navy. He was practicing a management style you might call "walking around."

Churchill didn't hold back. He made a habit of arranging interviews with junior officers and enlisted personnel. Top brass did not approve of his giving ear to every level of worker, but the practice served his purpose of gathering information. "He had a yarn with nearly all the lower deck men of the ship's company," the *Daily Express* newspaper wrote of a submarine visit in 1912, "asking why, wherefore, and how everything was done. All the sailors 'go the bundle' on him, because he makes no fuss and takes them by surprise. He is here, there, everywhere."[8]

Churchill's openness with officers and enlisted men was effective for gathering information, but it would not have been possible unless he was willing to take action based on his values. Despite pressure to be constrained by outdated social mores, he acted on his belief that the safety and success of the men was his priority. His intention was clear. In his role as first lord of the admiralty, he made no distinction among men. Instead, he made all men distinct.

Heroic Values

How our values shape our leadership can be seen in this one hero, Sir Winston Churchill, who placed a high value on what others had the potential to contribute. That value has won him an enduring place in the history of the world. This value was at the core of his talent for communicating. He won the trust of the Royal Navy, down to the last man. He imparted vision in his actions, and he exhibited clarity, commitment and energy. The value he placed on his organization meant more to him than the social expectations of English society or the management expectations of his fellow military leaders. His values—and his commitment to them—freed him to make the bold decisions that would contribute so magnificently to saving England from Hitler 25 years later. As first lord of the admiralty, his intention was to gain enterprise expertise. He was willing to put unprecedented interpersonal exchanges to work as the way to achieve meaningful success.

Churchill was a disciplined executive with increasing technical competence. But disciplined habits, executive skills, and technical competence do not, in and of themselves, make a successful leader. Leadership also requires personal values that provide a singular, inspiring image to help others find their own way through difficult times. Throughout his long career, Churchill's success was built on a foundation of heroic values that transcended the darkest days. Everything he communicated, and every manner in which he communicated, projected those values. He embodied them. What is less known, however, is how carefully he studied his own style, and how every statement and method of communicating was a conscious choice.

No matter how difficult the times, Churchill relied on honesty to drive transformation. He communicated what he thought and felt to those he believed would benefit from his message. He was open and clear, and was not known for sending hidden messages. People could trust what he said, even if they didn't like it. He offered his honest thoughts, ideas and feelings, and he shared his message directly with those for whom it was intended. None of his biographers writes about Churchill telling something to a third party and hoping the message would be passed along.

As a young man, Churchill had determined that he would "not shrink from stating the true facts to the public."[9] His commitment to honesty toward those who relied on him was unwavering. As prime minister in 1942, faced with mounting criticism about his handling of the war, Churchill demanded a formal vote of confidence in the House of Commons. "It is because things have gone badly, and worse is to come," he said, "that I demand a vote of confidence."[10] He did not want to presume to have the right to lead, and he did not want to retain his position of leadership by concealing the reality of difficult times. He prevailed, by a vote of 464 to 1. The nation that would eventually follow him to victory was galvanized by his honesty.

Churchill chose to deliver bad news personally, not only to the House of Commons but to the Allies as well. One of the toughest moments of the war for him was when it became apparent that the Allies could not open a second front against the Germans in 1943, as he had promised Stalin. Churchill went to Moscow to tell Stalin personally. "It was like taking a lump of ice to the North Pole," he said.[11]

Churchill meticulously critiqued his own communications. He carefully weighed the potential consequences of quoting other people lest he inadvertently spread gossip, with its dangerous impact on morale and trust. For the same reason, he guarded against attribution. He believed that attributing statements to others out of context could be misleading.

Priorities

Values help order our priorities and challenge us to act in ways that support them, although our actions may seem counterintuitive. Churchill's values and intention compelled him to walk around his navy. His priority of gaining the most and best information was served by his actions. In this one image, we see how his values, intention, goals and vision were integrated. They were clear and unified, so much so that it's hard sometimes to imagine how different the picture would have been if only one factor were changed. For example, consider how much less successful Churchill's leadership would have been throughout his life if his values did not permit him to mingle with people of lower social classes than his own. His historic success reveals the power of a leader who has internal integration.

Another core leadership value Churchill practiced was forgiveness. He wrote in 1921, "I do not harbor malice. I always forgive political attacks or ill-treatment not directed at private life."[12] He believed that people who were forced to pay a price for disagreeing with him or opposing him would hold back and not be as valuable to him in the future. His priority was to tap the best that everyone had to offer. He took the spiritual value of forgiveness to the highest strategic management level—international affairs.

Forgiveness was a strange core value for a politician. The new world reality Churchill faced as prime minister during World War II was one of treachery, and many leaders would have believed that the circumstances warranted ferocity even toward one's own colleagues. His nation's resources were growing short, and the environment was one of tumult and upheaval. He might have chosen to abide by Darwinian laws that enable only the most fit to survive through competition and dominance. (Many leaders today believe these are the compelling laws of the global marketplace, and this is the reasoning by which a significant number of leaders throughout history have lost sight of ethical values altogether.) But Churchill stayed focused on his priorities and stuck by his values.

As a result of his clarity and commitment, Churchill not only was forgiving but also took the time to express his forgiving attitude. Lord Bridges wrote after the war, "I cannot recollect a single minister, serving officer, or civil servant who was removed from office because he stood up to Churchill and told Churchill that he thought his policy or proposals were wrong."[13]

This practiced, disciplined forgiveness was most on display during the war. Because of his clear and consistent warnings over the previous years about Germany, Churchill's leadership position was invincible. If anyone had the right to say "I told you so" and to take retribution against officials who had opposed him, he did. But he did no such thing. In one instance, Churchill graciously accepted an apology from a conservative Member of Parliament who had tried to remove him from Parliament just a few months before the outbreak of war. Churchill's response was "I certainly think that Englishmen ought to start fair with one another from the outset in so grievous a struggle, and, so far as I am concerned, the past is dead."[14]

A forgiving attitude enabled this world leader to be very much a team player. Once a policy was set or a political quarrel decisively settled, Churchill would cease his opposition and get on board. In the early 1930s, after losing a long and bitter fight against India becoming a semi-independent dominion, Churchill told one of his opponents, "You need not expect anything but silence or help from us."[15] During the 1930s, the party leadership snubbed Churchill and scorned his advice. Nonetheless, he campaigned vigorously on behalf of party candidates during general elections.

His graciousness provided a role model for a nation whose very survival depended on its ability to unify against daunting odds. Churchill was serving his country in every detail of his choices.

Churchill also made deliberate choices about handling stress. His colleagues and friends marveled at how calm he was in the most trying circumstances. He had no silver-bullet solution; his primary method of dealing with stress and staying focused was never to be in a hurry. He projected calmness amid commotion and crisis. He was someone others could count on. His calmness imparted confidence and was the key to his enormous productivity.

But calm did not come naturally. Churchill cultivated calm as a discipline, because he remained true to his priorities. His belief was that hastiness would dilute his concentration, disrupt his priorities, and make it impossible for him to follow a consistent method of work. His tranquility and insistence on leisure time grounded his immense powers of concentration and were in many ways the linchpin of his success. Churchill understood what it meant to be on purpose, and he remained there.

Considering priorities, I'm reminded of Robert Sledd, chairman of Performance Food Group (a Fortune 500 company) and one of the thought leaders I've spoken with over the years. In an interview, Bob told me, "You can have too many priorities. It's important to focus on a handful of things. You can throw a hundred things on the board. They all look good. You have to prioritize and, optimally, focus on the top three. If you try to focus on too many things, it can be bad. I did that at first. I was like a kid in a candy store. There were so many things I wanted to do. But we ended up not doing any of them very well.... By getting focused, in 14 years, we went from $40 million to $2 billion in sales."

Communicating Meaning

Churchill is justifiably famous for providing meaning and direction to his country and the world in cataclysmic times. I learned about meaning at a young age, sitting around the kitchen table of our rented house with my parents and brothers. We learned that the meaning behind driving the old Chevy Impala was that we were working toward a greater goal—buying a house and starting a family business that would provide future security. A few years later, we celebrated together as we sat in the kitchen of our new house. Our collective intention had been realized. Our sense of accomplishment was integrated with our lives, because our parents took the time to communicate the real meaning of sacrifice and accomplishment.

Military leaders, especially, understand that communications must be clear without getting bogged down in detail or nuance. In the heat of battle, concise orders ensure survival. But when they're not in battle, military leaders manage large groups of highly trained and engaged people. As their challenges become more like those of a CEO than those of a battlefield commander, military leaders—like any executive—seek to achieve their goals with less direction and more motivation.

Everyone agrees that communication is essential for managing any large-scale effort, but not all leaders understand how to communicate meaning, and many of those who do had to learn it the hard way.

Bob Sledd talked to me about the idea of weathering big mistakes and finding wisdom where you might otherwise have only disaster. He said, "I'm committed to working with and through people. The people who report to me have people working with them. I believe in sitting down and creating a collective vision and moving forward together. That said, we all go through learning curves in life." Bob described a situation where not creating a collective vision turned into what he considered a disaster.

When he first assumed the leadership of his family-run corporation, Performance Food Group, he came to loggerheads with a long-time employee whose performance did not meet the requirements Bob defined. The man left, and Bob promoted someone else to take over. What he failed to do was to explain the change to the rest of the employees. He said, "I made a huge mistake. I didn't sit down with all the people and tell them all the reasons why I had promoted this new person, where we needed to go, how we were going to get there, and that the person I had promoted was the guy I believed could lead them to do it. Instead, I just promoted him. I asked him to explain his new position to his folks and to move forward. That was stupid on my part.... I've learned that you need to let people know where you're going and how you're going to get there if you have a bump in the road—*especially* if you have a bump in the road. You need to be able to lay that out even if it's going to involve some people losing their jobs. Looking back, if I had it to do over, I would have brought that new person in, and we would have developed a strategy for how to approach our people. He would have had a pretty good feeling for what was going on with them and what they were thinking. I would have been more of a coach to him and worked together with him to get the transition resolved and accepted. I think that he didn't know how to deal with the problem. Not that I did. But, together, I think we could have figured it out."

Years later, when Bob faced a similarly momentous change, he said he "got on the phone immediately.... We put together a message to associates and gave them a number they could call. We put out written communication to everyone. Basically, I explained to them what had happened, where we were, where we were going, and that we were going to be okay. I met with the senior management team to calm them down and met with the associates here to reassure everyone the sky wasn't falling." Bob had learned to communicate meaning, and to mean to communicate.

Trust

Bob also talked to me about returning as CEO of Performance Food Group a few years after leaving. His first order of business was to determine whom he could trust. "When I say trust," he said, "I mean if somebody tells me something, can I believe them? Do they really have their arms around the business? Are they really focused on the right things? If they told me they were, they needed to show me. When I went through a plan with an individual, I was asking myself if I was talking to the right individual. Or was someone else doing the work and they were just repeating what they are being told by the person doing the work? I was continuously asking myself if I needed to be talking to someone else in the organization to get the whole story."

Bob ended his story by describing how he had grown to a whole new level of effectiveness by earning the trust of his group. Trust is why people follow leaders—and what enables leaders to create environments in which everyone is empowered to work without fear of retribution. Taking the lesson from Winston Churchill, the only way to create a setting in which every contributor is free to participate is to create trust. And one of the best ways to create trust is to forgive mistakes and failures.

Churchill talked to people in every corner of his organization when he regularly walked around the Royal Navy. Ultimately, his honesty and willingness to communicate moved the whole nation to trust him. By forgiving mistakes and failures, he encouraged people to keep trying and contributing to the effort. In this way, he led a nation that was almost pummeled to death in the early years of World War II to transcendent victory.

Bob's openness about his own mistakes and learning curve has paid off for Performance Food Group. He said, "I'm amazed by the gap between where we started and where we are at this point. There are 3,000 distributors in the industry. Other than Sysco in 1969, no one has done it but us. A lot of folks have tried, but their egos got in the way. I'm not any smarter than the other guy. We had a lot of good people."

David Wright, chief operating officer of Capital One (Europe), has some specific ideas about the importance of being excited as a way to activate the highest potential in all the people on his teams. He noted the Second Law of Thermodynamics, which states that any system will decay if you don't put energy into it. David described actively seeking to access people's energy by looking for ways to get them excited and keep things fresh. "It's important to compel and excite people," he said. "I even change things that work. I don't want people or systems to stagnate."

As leaders, Bob Sledd and David Wright work with an attitude that might make many leaders quite uncomfortable. However, they are leaders in motion who understand the power that can be unleashed by a culture of transformation, in which the goal is to embrace mistakes because people are continuously asked to venture beyond what they know. These two leaders create cultures where mistakes are a valuable aspect of growth and success, and where attitudes toward mistakes reveal how successful we can be.

CHAPTER SIX

New Ways of Thinking

Where Mistakes Create Power and Value

Optimism is key to the can-do attitude essential for successful leadership. Unfortunately, most organizations suffer from inertia, which results in an it-can't-be-done attitude. The effort to overcome inertia often pits leaders against the organization—for a while.

The paralysis of pessimism was always unacceptable to Churchill. Clifford Jarrett, one of his aides, recalled that Churchill's "supreme talent was in goading people into giving up their cherished reasons for not doing anything at all."[16] For example, in 1939, when he was told of delays in shipbuilding, Churchill sent a memo to one of his senior administrators: "It is no use the contractors saying it cannot be done. I have seen it done when full pressure is applied, and every resource and contrivance utilised."[17]

Churchill's attitude was one of can-do optimism. "I am one of those," he remarked in 1910, "who believe that the world is going to get better and better."[18] Throughout his career, one of his favorite phrases was "All will come right." He repeated it often in the darkest days of World War II, and he seldom ended a wartime speech without a ringing note of optimism, usually drawn from an English poet. He ended one speech with a lyric from Arthur Hugh Clough: "But westward, look, the land is bright!"[19]

Churchill took his optimism a step further, deploring negative thinking and avoiding negative speech. Respectful of the burdens and challenges faced by those around him, he waged his battle against defeatism with gentle wit. In a speech to his officers in the trenches in France in 1916, Churchill exhorted, "Laugh a little, and teach your men to laugh. If you can't smile, grin. If you can't grin, keep out of the way till you can."[20]

In Bob Sledd's story of his experience leading Performance Food Group, I was struck by how, valuing his own mistakes as lessons, he was able to lead the company to greater accomplishments. Hearing about some of the tough spots he found himself in over the years reminded me again that clear intention provides the will and the way for success. Like most evolved leaders I've met, Bob understands the simple idea that "looking out from prison bars, one can see the mud or one can see the stars."

Bob and David Wright both concentrated on feeding their strength. In Bob's case, he was able to assess his work—including his mistakes—clearly because he refrained from judgment and simply paid attention. David talked about being willing to "trip, stumble, learn and grow as part of our expansion.... We must observe our own performance and get feedback, coaching, and help from other people."

Attitude is the starting point for success. Like the image of a skier on a coin, how we think about the journey before us influences our final destination. Our personal transformational process relies on a change in the way we think about mistakes, failures, excuses and stressors. The new thinking we need is one that puts the choice of success squarely on our shoulders. We begin by cultivating an attitude that will keep us in motion through all the cycles of learning we will encounter as we transform and grow.

Mistakes

Our attitude about mistakes helps define us. In many cases, we're taught that mistakes are bad, and we may even be punished for making them. It's hard to unlearn that way of thinking. And yet, humans are designed to learn by making mistakes. We learn to walk by falling down. If we never fell down, we'd never walk. I learned to ski because I learned how to fall—and how to fail.

If I know what I want, I have clear intention. With clear intention, I can find the way to move (or ski) mountains. But clear intention does not guard against mistakes. Mistakes are a necessary part of the cycle of learning. In fact, clear intention may increase the risk of making mistakes.

Changes in how we think do not change the external realities. Attitude is not about delusion. A great attitude cannot make a challenge smaller or the mountain less daunting. What a great attitude does is enable me to try without the fear of failure. It postures my thinking for success, and that's something I can offer to others once I've mastered it myself. My attitude can boost the success of others as well as my own.

In the relentless pursuit of excellence, successful leaders come to see mistakes as opportunities to gain wisdom for future success. Our attitudes about our mistakes and failures, our successes and achievements play a role in how useful mistakes can be in our evolution. A starting point is whether we exercise the power of choice not only before we make a mistake but also after—when we choose the attitude with which we will interpret it. Failing to win has two meanings, and only one meaning makes failure a bad thing.

Fear of failure holds us back mentally, spiritually and emotionally. It interrupts a natural cycle of learning, limiting our growth and development. Giving up because they're worn down by the fear of failing keeps millions of people stuck in a rut every day. They are too afraid of their negative fantasies to take a leap of faith. Winners are not afraid of losing. They don't *like* losing, but they've learned how to handle it. Winners make choices about what they want and summon the courage to take the risks to go for it, even in the face of fear and uncertainty. They're willing to fail in order to win. That's the winning attitude.

Failure

There are mistakes, and there is failure. Looking at the failures that have changed the course of our lives can be so hard for people that I usually start the discussion by recounting a devastating failure in my own life. This failure was the source of my biggest lesson in how attitude equals success. It happened when I failed my preliminary exams in graduate school.

There's always a context in which we fail. For me, it was that I had left my family short on help to pursue my own dreams. They still had to raise food crops, and my dad was just beginning to build a business that promised to provide more financial security for the family. First I worked in a restaurant and a grocery store to save some money for school, then I left to go to school. Success in school had become the way I assuaged my guilt for leaving my family to struggle a little harder in a lean existence. Every new level of education I achieved was a way of thanking my family and assuring myself that their sizable sacrifice was not in vein. Every failure affects more than one person.

I was accustomed to hard work leading to success. Before progressing from my master's studies to a doctoral program, I had to pass preliminary exams, in which my knowledge of my field would be assessed. Preparation for me and my fellow students was grueling, and I studied for months in advance of the test. But I wasn't worried, because I was accustomed to hard work producing success. Two days of written testing were followed by an oral exam. I felt confident as I answered all the questions and—as I waited for the final decision from the exam committee—confident of the outcome. It was into this state of ignorant bliss that the jarring news crashed: I had failed the exams. I was too shocked to feel ruined—that would come later. First, I had to go to a party.

I left the campus and headed to a party thrown by friends to celebrate my passing the prelims. I stood numb, as if at a funeral, as friends and relatives who knew about the result offered condolences. Some people stammered in surprise when they heard the news; some slunk out of the party. My failure was frightening to my peers. Failing prelims was unheard of, and they knew me as a hard worker. For the remainder of that awful day, keeping a smile on my face at the party distracted me from the reality that I had failed at something very important. It was my first huge failure.

The next day, the implications of the failure shook me. If I tried again, I'd lose a year of my life and would have to repeat the exhausting study period and the grueling tests—with the possibility of failing again. If I didn't try again, I would not progress on to a doctorate. I wanted the degree. I needed it to be competitive in my field. I needed to pass this test if I wanted to move forward toward my goals. But even though the choice was obvious, it seemed impossible. I quickly devolved to feeling like the depressed victim of circumstance.

Before I could collect my wits and make a good decision, I had to face something that had not ever been part of my self-image: failure. Not only had I failed, but I quickly sank into thinking that I *was* a failure. I thought of my family's support when I went to work for my education, leaving them to manage without me. Now I'd have to admit to them that their sacrifice had been for nothing. My imagination began to run wild. (This was before I understood that I had a choice about how to use my imagination—for seeing the best or the worst outcomes.)

My entire self-image came into question, and the failure loomed larger and larger. The only outcome I could see was that I would not complete what I had set out to do and I would not recover from this crushing blow. I wanted to hide in a closet and never come out again. That was the second day. Several days passed. Something had to change.

My failure—and the possibility that I would fail twice—caused me to rethink my life goals and my mission on the planet. But the real question was what I was going to do about this failure, right now. In the days following the crushing blow, I thought about how long I'd wanted to be a psychologist and how hard I'd worked to succeed.

Before I could start learning from my failure, I had to get back to my intention. Intention restored me to my original course and gave me the will to try again. Where there's intention, there's a way. I started to see that this failure might be life-changing and that the change could be for the better, if I chose. I saw that I could decide whether or not the failure defined me and what I might learn from it. The first priority was clear immediately: The only way to be who I wanted to be was to take the prelims again—and pass them. I knew what I wanted, so I started to find a way.

When my advisor emerged from the committee meeting a few days earlier to inform me of the disastrous results, she had offered important feedback, but I was too shocked to process it at the time. Now I was ready to focus on the specific concerns of the committee, to return to my advisor and ask her advice. Together, we began to consider the options that would let me press through this difficult challenge.

My advisor, Roseanne Foti, was my mentor at a watershed moment in my life. She took the time to help me walk through the process of turning this failure into success. She guided me to solutions by clearly and calmly assessing the test answers I'd given and helping me figure out better ways to show my command of an area that I understood but was not yet articulating well. With compassion and respect, she showed me how to walk the path from failure to strength. She knew—as I was learning—that failure could lead to success and that I could gain much from this catastrophe. I had made the first, most important choice: not to let a failure make *me* a failure.

Starting Point

I learned that failures and mistakes can be dead ends or they can be starting points. Whether they are one or the other depends entirely on our attitudes and our choices. It is a singular moment in life and in our careers when we accept responsibility for our attitudes and choices, and the impact they have on our lives.

Roseanne and I devised a plan for me to enroll in an internship program that would provide a change of venue and expand my horizons. In other words, I committed to continue growing even as I overcame the setback. After an internship with BellSouth Corporation in Atlanta, Georgia, I would return to school in time to study for the next round of preliminary exams.

As a result of this strategy, I found myself in a business setting that was to have a huge influence on my career, where I had my first clear sense of what I wanted to do with my professional life. I worked with a team of interns who had all passed their prelims. Being with them was a constant reminder of my pitiful performance, but they were the source of constant inspiration as well. I often cried myself to sleep and dreaded going back to school to repeat the Herculean task of studying for months for a test I might fail again. At the same time, though, I gained a sense of peace about my decision.

After about a year at BellSouth, it was time to return to school and study for the exam—or retreat into my comfort zone. Feelings of self-pity came and went. I wanted to blame everything and everyone but myself, but I knew if I tried again and failed, I'd have only myself to blame. The decision was about whether I was ready to accept responsibility for my attitude and choices. It was a life-changing moment, a starting point. I returned to school.

As I began to study, I was pleasantly surprised to realize that my professors and classmates were 100 percent supportive. My efforts were not judged harshly by anyone but myself. At times, I became discouraged and wondered if I should drop out. I had a terrible fear of failing again. But colleagues were quick to encourage me and to offer helpful hints on ways I could improve my study habits. Their suggestions and feedback started to have an impact.

In this supportive environment, it took only a few weeks to realize that there was indeed a lot I didn't know. I looked with fresh eyes at the committee's feedback, and I studied with renewed vigor, but I was still fighting panic. How would I learn all this material? Could I do it? Over the months, I gained knowledge from studying. Moreover, my understanding of myself and others seemed to expand.

The memory of the struggle remains vivid today. In fact, it took a long time before I could even bring myself to talk about this experience openly. But, like Bob Sledd, I know that even the most jarring failures are important starting points. One of the most valuable lessons I learned was how, when we've failed at something important, we learn how difficult it can be to move beyond the impact. That's the first lesson of failure; through it, we become more seasoned and better able to respect others' failures.

At the end of six months, I had become self-assured and prepared as an expert in my field. I took the prelims again, and this time I passed. If I'd let fear win the battle for how I chose to respond to my initial failure, it would have taken control over all my future decisions and actions. My power to make a difference in the world around me would have been stunted.

The story seems to end here, but it does not. The power of this choice has stayed with me throughout my career. How I chose to respond to failure did, indeed, define me. All the subsequent growth in my ongoing process of personal mastery and transformational leadership has been based on the willingness I Iearned during that period of crisis. The most valuable lesson was to value my mistakes and failures and to find in them starting points for levels of success I hadn't thought were attainable. For me, failure unleashed unimagined possibilities in a way uninterrupted success could not have done.

Blaming

Most barriers to our goals lie within us. They are internal and are revealed in the process of mastering ourselves through honesty and authentic transformation.

For a short and terrible time, failing my preliminary exams had a vise grip on my self-image, confidence and hope for the future. I had a good long bout with self-pity, which continued as long as I kept blaming outside factors for the failure. When I took responsibility for the failure, I was able to get back on a path to success. Now I see blaming as an escape from reality.

It's human nature to blame external factors for inadequate outcomes. When I find myself blaming outside forces for my inferior performance, it's a signal to me that I need to examine my stated intention versus my demonstrated intention. When I failed my prelims, I blamed a lot of people and things, including my committee, my background, and my work responsibilities. But once I gained clarity that I would take the test again and pass it, I found a way to do it. My attitude had shifted to a winning one.

A few years after this momentous failure in my life, I would stand at the edge of a 300-foot precipice in my Bunny slope skis with none of the skill needed to make the jump. It didn't take long for me to see that I could keep standing there yelling downhill or that I could follow advice from an experienced skier, take off my skis and climb backwards down the steep slope. The choice was mine to make and mine to live.

Choice

Attitude is the starting point for turning all our outcomes, successful or not, into learning experiences that lead to higher levels of success. Attitude is at the core of transformation. It is, above all, about making the same choice over and over. It's worth challenging ourselves to make better choices about attitude. How far are we willing to go?

We can see the glass as half empty and choose a victim outlook, which means living at the mercy of daily events; hoping that health, wealth and happiness will be delivered to our doorsteps. If we choose the role of victim, our self-image is one of lucky winner or injured party, depending on the situation. When things go wrong, we have the convenient option of blaming other people, outside factors or fate. We have the easy out of believing that what happens to us is beyond our control. We float from one incident to another, with no sense of direction or purpose—sometimes feeling persecuted, sometimes feeling lucky. We're off the hook—not responsible for our attitude or decisions. We are powerless victims of fate. If we adopt this attitude, life is reduced to a series of reactions.

When I failed my prelims, I came face to face with the impulse to blame my failures on others. But with help and by looking within, I came to realize that the glass was more than half full of opportunity. I now cultivate this attitude and use it to create the results I choose. I see myself as accountable for making things happen around me and for seizing opportunities. As an example, I've chosen to redefine how I think and feel about my tobacco-farming years. I've rewritten that script. Instead of dwelling on the hardship aspect, I realize that farming was a chance to learn how to be patient, to grow things, to organize work and people, and to implement a plan to create desired results. In fact, what I know about growing tobacco, vegetables and flowers makes me a much more effective consultant and professional. The same is true for having failed my prelims the first time around. I've tapped all the good there was to find in that experience.

What is the moral of this story? Sometimes I win, and sometimes I learn. My fear of failure is real, but that's not the problem that can undermine my success. The greatest challenge to my growth and evolution is how I *handle* fear and failure. How I choose to think determines whether, ultimately, I will succeed or fail.

Holding a proper attitude toward failure and success makes the difference in my life. My failures have made me stronger and smarter, especially when I've been able to take the losses and turn them into victories. As I said earlier, we can't walk down the road of life holding hands with comfort while we also grow. We must choose.

I chose to face my fears rather than giving up on what I wanted my life to be. We need to realize that we can't hide in a closet and at the same time shine our light. As leaders, our efforts to know our core selves and to challenge ourselves to grow are how we start to shed light on the circumstances and people around us. This is the basis from which we begin to develop "people mastery"—the ability to create and sustain purposeful, meaningful relationships. People mastery, unlike personal mastery, requires us to look outward and commit to a conscious intention to work with others' ideas, needs, concerns and feelings.

Good Stress

One of the most important decisions we make in life has to do with choosing how we handle stress. We are surrounded by stress. In fact, we're struggling to survive in the midst of a stress epidemic. The same is true for the people working with us and for us. Stress is our collective milieu.

Lack of role clarity, maddening traffic, multitasking, living beyond one's means, rising costs, a troubled economy, too much caffeine, no exercise, unhealthy eating habits, not enough sleep—these are some of the stressors people face each day.

Combine all these stress factors, and the result is people who are not at their best. Add the sense that they have no power over their circumstances, and you have increasingly stressed, unhealthy and off-balance people showing up at work. In that state of mind, a person will succumb to bad decision making, low productivity, impatience, lethargy and irritability. Multiply this effect from one person to a team—or even the majority of people in an organization—and you have a systemic problem.

A person's choices—or lack of choices—can kick off a cycle of negative energy that depletes the group rather than contributing to it. If that person is you, the leader, the problem is compounded. Leaders are especially influential in the work environment. One great impact we can have is whether people work under extremely stressful circumstances or—if we are the antidotes to stress—they're ready and able to contribute their best.

If we fail to make choices that reduce stress, we undermine our capacity for focus and mindfulness. Centered choices are a cornerstone of personal mastery, and they ensure the most effective evolution for the group and for the person—including you.

Recommendations that people must make choices to reduce stress seem to be falling on deaf ears, however. Considering statistics for diseases related to hypertension, heart disease, and stroke by the U.S. Centers for Disease Control and Prevention, 50 percent of deaths before the age of 65 are due to stressful lifestyles. Research from the American Institute of Stress calculates that 75–90 percent of all visits to primary care physicians are for stress-related illnesses.[21] Do statistics like these indicate that we need to stamp out stress? Not exactly. The stress we experience on a daily basis is part of life—people have been stressed throughout history. What is critical is how we *handle* stress. How we choose to manage stress determines whether we feel overwhelmed or in control. Our ability to grow is supported or undermined by how we handle stress. Whether we can be healthy or not is affected by how we choose to respond to stress.

How can we think about living less stressful lives so we can be more effective? Can we focus on the primary decision at the heart of the matter? If so, we may be able to make progress where progress has been hard to make.

Walter Cannon, a physiologist at Harvard University, coined the term *fight or flight* around 1900. Fight or flight describes a set of physiological changes that are a natural response to danger. When we feel threatened, our bodies prepare us to defend ourselves or to run as fast as we can to safety. We either fight or flee. The details of the fight or flight response are well known, and our reactions in high stress situations are stunningly similar. For example, during the fight or flight response, our vision and hearing sharpen. Pain-killing endorphins flood the body to put us in peak condition to face the challenge. Blood flow is redirected to our muscles to ensure rapid responses. Our breathing quickens, along with our heart rate. Stress hormones such as adrenaline and cortisol are activated, and our sense of alertness goes on "high." Sugar and fatty acids flood out of storage into the bloodstream to give us a surge of energy beyond what we would normally have. To support this focus on survival, other systems are dialed down or suspended: the immune systems, restorative healing processes, digestion, and sex drive. We're ready to fight or run. The problem is that we're just sitting at a desk or behind the wheel of a car. We're on the kind of high alert our ancestors needed in the wild, but this isn't what we need 10 minutes before a big meeting or in the middle of a major decision.

When you find yourself on high alert sitting at your desk or in your car, the first step is to understand that the flight or fight response is a choice. In nature, certain instincts take over as you respond to danger and choose the right option—flee or fight. But this is the 21st century, and you're not facing a saber-toothed tiger. The faster you can identify the fight or flight response and avoid pumping unneeded adrenaline through your body, the more appropriately you'll be able to respond to the reality around you. As leaders, we must be able to override instinct when we ask others to work in a competitive setting, or we'll be feeding the tension and reactivity, not freeing those around us from responding to the day's challenges with the reactions of cave dwellers.

Leaders can model how to choose tools to reduce psychic stress so work proceeds in a constructive manner. Each of us is free to choose whether to yell at the person stalled in traffic in front of us or to put relaxing music on the radio and practice calm breathing. Think about Winston Churchill. He had some serious stressors to deal with, and he chose calm.

Calm is a choice. Stress is a choice.

The more we consciously choose to evolve beyond outdated behaviors, the more we can see that life's common stress factors do not warrant fighting or running. We learn that we can choose a positive attitude over a negative attitude toward stress. It all comes back to attitude.

The fight or flight response can be kicked off by any stressor—positive or negative. But there is a crucial difference in brain functioning related to positive stress (the challenges that mobilize and motivate us) compared with that related to negative or bad stress (the threats that overwhelm, paralyze or demoralize us). The brain chemicals that generate enthusiasm for a challenge are different from those that generate fear of a threat. And in many cases, whether we experience enthusiasm or fear is a matter of choice. We can choose attitudes that challenge, motivate and mobilize us, and that bring out the best in us. In other words, we can circumvent the fight or flight impulse by choosing to feel neither. How? By changing how we think.

Studies show that people who choose to meet stressors with a positive attitude develop a remarkable hardiness and can bear the physical burden of stress much better. They emerge from difficult times with far less illness. Their hardiness permits them, despite stress, to stay committed, feel in control, and be challenged.

So, the truth is that we can choose to be resilient. We can choose to become hardy.

Consider the person who has long-standing habits that promote negative stressors in his life. He lacks focus and commitment. He feels out of control and stressed most of the time. He may even seek out stressful situations, becoming an "adrenaline junkie." Avoiding all stressors may seem saner, but if he does that he's probably not committing to personal growth. In either case, this person will not be able to evolve freely with a growing organization. If he connects well with people, he'll transfer his tendency toward stress or entrenchment to others. He will not be able to unite people, and he'll be a drain on the group's energy, not a source of inspiration. The ability to unite and channel the energy of a group depends on the ability to be consistently resilient or hardy.

This all goes back to the basic commitment to consciously master ourselves through authentic effort, honesty and evolution. In my firm's coaching and training sessions, one of the hardest things we do is to help participants see the obvious—that they have a choice about how they interpret and respond to the stimuli, people, troubles and challenges around them. Choices directly affect outcomes.

Breakthroughs come at all levels. One major breakthrough is when people are able to perceive feedback not as something to fear but as a gift to seek on a continuous basis in order to help them be more effective. This is one way people begin to see mistakes and failures as starting points. They slow down enough to challenge their own reactions and to change the small behaviors that can have such an adverse effect on the work environment. They start to experiment more with less fear.

Whether or not we will have a fear response depends on two factors. One is physiological arousal, and the other is thoughts that interpret a situation as threatening and then attribute our physiological arousal to fear. The key to unlocking this hidden cycle is to remember that the actual situation often has little to do with our emotional response. The way our thoughts interpret the stimulus and the feeling we have is the real force behind whether the stress we experience is negative (draining our resources for a fight or flight response) or positive (energizing and motivating us).

This explains why the same person who is exhilarated by skydiving leaps onto a chair shaking and shrieking in terror when she sees a mouse on the floor or gets angry when her boyfriend serves her chocolate cake. In all three situations, she experiences the fight or flight response, but she attributes it to three different emotions. In the first case, skydiving, she labels her physical sensations as excitement. In the second case, seeing a mouse, she remembers being bitten by a small animal as a child and labels her reaction as fear. In the third case, the chocolate cake, she believes her boyfriend has been thoughtless because he knows she's allergic to chocolate; so she labels her reaction as anger.

Hard as it may seem to believe, we are capable of choosing to label feelings differently. We can look at stimuli—at stressors—differently and have different responses. Eventually, we learn how to choose so our bodies don't click into a fight or flight response at all.

For example, our skydiver can look at her fear of mice and stop playing the old tape from the past. She can set some traps or hire an exterminator. She can discover her own power where she used to feel out of control. Regarding the chocolate cake, the skydiver can examine her expectations for how much people are supposed to remember about her food allergies. She can communicate more clearly the things she wants people close to her to remember and maybe practice forgiveness when they don't.

When we take responsibility for our assumptions, we begin to break the cycle of stress and become free to face seeming threats with energy and enthusiasm. All that's required is a conscious mental shift in how we view our world. All that's required is a change in attitude.

Kicking the Habit

With a change in attitude, we can kick bad habits, including one of the most insidious habits of all: the modern stress habit. The modern habit of stress harms us in many ways. It undermines the capacity of leaders to be alert, flexible and responsive. To kick any habit, we must cultivate conscious behavioral shifts. Our new thinking leads us to new ways of behaving. We're beginning to model transformation for those with whom we work.

The first step for many of us to become more productive as leaders seems counterintuitive, and it's a hard step to take. The more our stress habit is embedded in the way we choose to live, the harder it will be to kick it. The first step is to allow more time to release our tension and fully relax.

I've talked about how Winston Churchill inspired his nation to persevere to triumph against seemingly overwhelming odds and inspired people to seek rejuvenation in creative endeavors such as art. He probably acquired this wisdom experientially, as a result of the many extremely tense and stressful events in his life. After great stress, release and relaxation are natural. In primitive societies, people played games after hunts—it was part of their cycle of adrenaline and release. Strong family and social networks in past societies provided support and refuge that are not as available in the more solitary routines and lives of the 21st century.

We must find ways to release tension and relax on a regular basis, so our bodies can flush away the physiological impact of the fight or flight response, and our minds can move out of that single-minded focus of adrenaline and into a more flexible, curious and open mode. Without a relaxation routine, we allow chronic stress in our lives and work patterns, and we lose the capacity for reflection, awareness and conscious evolution. In addition, we attract illnesses linked to chronic stress, such as heart attacks, high blood pressure, rheumatoid arthritis, ulcerative colitis, asthma, and migraine headaches. What goes on in our minds affects what goes on in our bodies—and in the world surrounding us.

In spite of what we know about its negative effects, chronic stress has become an unconscious national habit and a habit for many persons who are called upon to lead others. We do not take enough vacations. We reward each other for burning the candle at both ends. Movie and television characters make it seem normal to live life with chronic stress. And many of us enjoy the exhilarating rush of endorphins that accompanies the stress response. Our habituation to stress is so complete, so taken for granted, that we don't even question it. We accept it uncritically. As leaders, when we tolerate the habit in ourselves, the impact is far-reaching. We are modeling stress habits to those around us, withholding permission for people to reduce stress in their lives, and essentially rewarding anyone who builds stress and relays it among colleagues. Being a leader in motion is not the same as being a leader in a constant state of anxiety. The two are, in fact, polar opposites.

We can kick the stress habit by reestablishing the traditional stress cycle in our lives. That can be as simple as remembering to relax and take care of ourselves, which requires increasing levels of awareness. Sometimes stress is the direct result of little daily habits. Many times we can tolerate the downward drag of these habits because we're not forced to grow; or we may be unaware of them, even though we're unhappy because of their impact on our lives. The more consciously we choose to live, the more stressful outdated habits become. The more we evolve, the more some habits will become outdated. When we choose to face down the simple daily behaviors that create stress, we're choosing a life of serenity.

Courage

Fear is a common reaction to change. It plays a role in the fight or flight response. If we're in the forest and we see a bear, the fight or flight instinct has a role to play—it's not just a vestige of the past. Fear, too, has an important role—it can be a good instinctive read of some circumstances. More often, though, it holds us back from moving out of our comfort zones and into fresh ways of thinking and being that will open us to possibilities we haven't dared to imagine.

The best way to disarm the power of fear is to acknowledge it and just keep moving forward. That's easier said than done. But if we choose to believe in our ability to rebound, if we've adjusted our thinking about mistakes and failures, then we can also make decisions that catapult us forward beyond the worst we can imagine.

Elizabeth Murphy is vice president of professional services for Datatel, an award-winning software and services firm for higher education. When I spoke with Liz, she had some powerful insights into fear connected with an experience of dramatic change at Datatel. Under her leadership, an organizational overhaul was courageously conceived and implemented by the very people who would be most affected by its impact.

In response to a radical strategic change in client service philosophy, Datatel was undertaking a complete overhaul of its organizational structure. Liz knew that her group would undergo significant change. She said, "I decided to abandon myself to what comes from the people who are doing the work, and it was an insightful and powerful experience. I just believed in the people and, at the end of the day, I was amazed."

Liz went to an offsite gathering of the leaders in her group, having consciously chosen not to have any preconceived notions of what the new organization would look like or how it would work. What she heard was an inspiring, visionary solution, imagined collectively by the group. She was motivated to find a way to make what they were visualizing happen. A cycle of clarity, commitment and energy was beginning between this group of leaders and the woman who led them.

Liz took it to the next level. The members of her group challenged their peers at the director and senior management levels to participate in the transformation they envisioned. People started energizing each other. With each persuasive conversation, more clarity and commitment were built. The group was galvanizing and gaining momentum. Transformation was under way.

Many leaders might have taken a step back at that point, knowing what was next. Liz knew that the new structure would upend most jobs. Positions would be dramatically redefined—or eliminated. That meant that every contributor to the process would face personal risk as the momentum built. But she remained clear about the overall goal, convinced of her group's power, and energized by everyone's contributions to the process.

Liz recalls a defining meeting, a point of commitment. Could this group—which had designed a visionary organization, poised for the future in technology—accept the next obvious steps? She asked, "How many of you think this is the right thing for the customer?" Everyone agreed that it was. "How many of you are scared to death about what it means for you?" Everyone admitted that they were. They had all admitted their fear, and they were ready to keep moving forward.

In the end, this courageous group of leaders redesigned all the management positions to match the new organization they had envisioned; at the same time, they embarked on honest reflections about their own careers. They began to play back to Liz how the new jobs were new opportunities for people inside the company as well as talent from outside. Fully committed to the success of the overall vision, they were able to match people to positions with a vigor and honesty that, in the end, created fabulous solutions for everyone involved.

Liz recalls, "I was really awestruck by what was happening, and I had really given them very few parameters. I told them what the objective was. I gave them some general time frames. Then they began to talk about why, what was critical about the role and why their work team product was so critical. They made the decision that anybody who wanted to be part of the new management team would apply. People could apply for multiple positions, because we had lots of new ones. They would actually have to turn in a resume and a cover letter, and that was just scandalous to some people. They said, 'Liz, we don't understand why some people are threatened.' I said, 'Help them understand that we're trying to see them differently, and unless we have something fresh in front of us, we only see them for what they do now.' What happened was, we had a lot of people who didn't like what they were doing at all, and this caused them to say, 'If

I could do anything, what would I do?' What was most amazing was that the people who seemed unhappiest with their performance over the last three years that preceded this process self-selected into other jobs in the company or left, and we never had to have a hard conversation about it. And some of them were on the committee! It was incredibly magical."

She went on, "There was this other group of people who said, 'It's true, we have three internal candidates for this job, but we don't think any of them are the right people for the job. This job is too important and we don't have the right skills. Let's go outside.' So by the time we finished ... everybody was in a job that excited them, that they chose, that they knew the rest of the team had confidence in them to do. Some of these people went through 15 interviews, and they'd been working here 10 years, because everybody needed to see them in a different light. And even the people who decided to opt for jobs outside the division said it was the best-planned, most thoughtful and considerate management restructuring or change process they'd ever been through."

Liz's closing comments make a very important point: "There are times when I'm the boss, but the majority of the time, I'm not. It's hard when you have a large organization to have people look at you as an equal player in conversation. I think leadership vulnerability is important." This leader was courageous, taking as many steps forward into trusting her group as it would allow, and her group repaid her with courage beyond her imagining.

The Cycle of Learning

As Liz Murphy's powerful story shows, it takes courage to participate in transformation. Another way of looking at it is that learning is an act of courage.

I laugh when I recount stories about misadventures that have led me to precipices; sometimes—like on my first ski trip—literally. Those are the times when I've found the personal resources to get up and try again. They're examples of how the cycle of learning works, if you go the full distance. The cycle of learning has to come full circle to have transforming power in our lives. We need to understand how it works and how we can cooperate with it.

When we first experience something new, we're facing the unknown. Our reactions reveal what we truly feel about the unknown, about mystery. Most people feel uncomfortable dealing with mystery. It's natural to reach for the familiar. So our first instinct is to jump back into our comfort zone. Often the leap is so fast we don't even notice that we did it.

Our comfort zone is safe and cozy. Being open to a new lesson is risky. It takes a conscious effort to open up and be honest with ourselves when we're venturing forward into new challenges that highlight our need to learn and grow. We can find a lot of reasons not to grow just yet. It's always reasonable to grow tomorrow.

Another pitfall is that even when we know we're choosing to retreat to our comfort zone, we give in to the impulse to think the challenge through again. We believe that if we can analyze the scary step long enough, we can somehow break free of our resistance. This usually just leads to indefinite procrastination. We focus on the boundaries of our comfort zone and anticipate the inevitable discomfort of crossing them. It's a circular trap with little or no forward motion. This is not the circular pattern you want to cultivate in your transformation. To break free of your comfort zone, you must take the risk. You must give up the idea that you can ever talk yourself out of discomfort. You must step out and allow yourself to feel uncomfortable.

Enduring the discomfort of venturing into unknown territory is the first step in the cycle. When I was faced with the need to get back on the ski slopes, with my lucky coin in my pocket, I came to a fork in the road. If I'd returned to my comfort zone, I wouldn't know how to ski now. I would have missed the lessons, the experiences, and the great memories of that very first trip.

Visualization is an important part of venturing forward into new challenges. Besides discomfort (even fear), you'll encounter excitement and new vistas. When you ski down a snowy slope with confidence, you feel alive, awake and alert. The same is true when we achieve a level of mastery over anything, including ourselves. The heightened consciousness travels with us far beyond the slopes of the early challenges. The effects are cumulative. As we take away the best of our lessons, we become ever more prepared to learn effectively in the future.

Visualizing how success feels helps us confront the next hurdle—the one high-achieving leaders dislike most. Our comfort zone is defined by what we know, including the limits of our expertise and capacity for personal mastery. When we take a risk, our performance often gets worse. One day we feel as though we're at the pinnacle of success; the next day we're facing a challenge that is beyond what we know at the moment. Our discomfort level rises and our confidence may be shaken. At this point, we must keep in mind that a dip in performance is part of the learning process; our performance will improve as we learn. Dips in performance are essential in the cycle of learning.

For those of us who are willing to stick with it, the reward is great. We gain insight and have life-changing breakthroughs. Later, with practice and feedback, we can sustain and expand our new knowledge. The cycle of learning is incorporated into our way of life. It becomes the way we work, and the way we encourage others to work. It lies at the core of transformation—in ourselves and in the world around us.

With the cycle of learning, one step evolves into a process, one risk and one decision at a time. Each time we choose to master a new level of skill or grow in a new area, we venture out, endure discomfort, make mistakes and conquer yet another mountain. The cycle builds confidence in ourselves and compassion for others. No one who is growing is perfect.

When I first learned to ski, I went through a wide range of feelings in one week, as my skill advanced through the levels. And every time I want to learn something new, I must work through this same range of feelings and move through many levels of effectiveness all over again. Even with skiing, when I decide to master the Double Black Diamond slopes, I know I'll have to get out of my comfort zone, take a risk, and possibly travel on my backside partway down a mountain or two.

The cycle of learning is the way we evolve as people, as leaders and as organizations. Our potential is phenomenal. Possibilities exceed what we can imagine. To tap one and enjoy the other, we must have intention. When the cycle of learning becomes our comfort zone, we'll know that evolution is becoming second nature for us, that we've chosen to let transformation become a way of life.

CHAPTER SEVEN

Practicing New Reactions
Transformational Tactics for Everyday Life

As personal transformation proceeds, we begin to encounter old ways of being and familiar ways of working which are no longer effective. We can become uncomfortable in our old mode of behavior and reactions. It is time to create and practice new ones.

We began with the understanding that organizational transformation is based on personal transformation. We understood that to master the enterprise we lead and the interpersonal connections around us, we must first master ourselves. As we learned more about ourselves by diving deep and being honest, we began to evolve, consciously challenging ourselves to make new choices about attitudes and habits. As we evolved toward continuous transformation in ourselves, we were also creating a culture of transformation around us.

Practicing new reactions is the tactical phase of personal mastery. Our work behaviors include many reactions that have long gone unchallenged because they have served us well. At one time, these reactions may have been new breakthroughs from old ways of being.

The process of adopting new behaviors never ends. It's a way of life. The need for new attitudes and changed habits is never fully resolved as long as we're growing into the future, evolving into ever higher levels of being. Learning how to practice new reactions is an essential element of transformation.

As we make changes in our personal behavior and presentation, we lead the way for others to make similar choices. We must model new reactions to others if we want them to find new ways to react to us, to each other, and to the challenges we share. That's how a process of personal mastery directs evolution around us from within us. To drive change deeper into the organization, we begin a process of bringing new reactions into our connections with those who seek our leadership.

How do we do this?

Personal mastery is an evolutionary process. As we make conscious choices to evolve and to embrace change, we become freer to respond with clarity, commitment and energy to the circumstances around us—they have an impact on us, and we on them. Our reactions may have settled into a circular rut. When we start to identify the reactions that fall short of true mastery, we can practice new, better ones. This is one way our work on personal mastery leads us out of the solitude of our reflections and back into the cycles of energy, growth and learning we can both inspire and learn from.

As we consciously challenge our attitudes and values, it makes sense that we must practice new reactions. The old habits born of outdated thinking do not change easily. It takes practice. One of the things we must practice is forgiveness—especially self-forgiveness—as we turn mistakes into starting points. Our process of self-mastery grows more and more tactical. What habits must be changed—and how? How can we better interact with people around us as a leader among equals?

Evolution is stressful because it comes up against some of our oldest impulses. We can choose, however, not to be stressed. We can choose to embrace the struggle to change our reactions in a positive new direction. We can visualize the positive results of our efforts and embrace the process of imperfect progress.

But we cannot change the fact that we must continue to change. As we grow more honest with ourselves and our consciousness expands, we bump into things we've long ignored that hold us back. As our personal mastery advances, we must tackle issues at the core of our own lives as professionals. The more responsibility we have, the more likely we face habits related to stress and fear that undermine the quality of our time and our work—and the time and work of those who depend on us for leadership.

Often, the first impulse when work performance is down, or we know we'll be guiding groups of people through transition or radical change, is to look outward. Actually we should look inward first, to see how our own reactions will play a role in the goals we set. The dynamic people with whom I work usually have a good feel for when it's time to stop digging into the core and start practicing new reactions. Time to change how they think, what they value, how they work, how they connect with people, how they manage frustration, how they learn, and what they expect from life. Changing those habits means changing their way of being intelligent. So, who is a leader? You are a leader, if you choose to be.

Time Is Precious

Our relationship with time is very important. Here lies an opportunity to examine and adjust our effectiveness. Sometimes we procrastinate, which undermines our ability to be effective. At the other extreme, we may almost kill ourselves with To Do lists worthy of a division of specialists. Invariably, we tell ourselves we'll just have to make the time to get it all done.

But there is no such thing as "making time."

We cannot make more time. Time is limited. Time is precious. When we talk about making time to get things done, we're not being honest with ourselves. We're perpetuating the illusion that we can squeeze more into one day than is possible. This is a good way to become stressed out and ineffective.

Time is a limited resource to be managed with care, especially if we're committed to the self-care that offsets stress. The best way to use limited time is to become more efficient. Efficiency is a choice. More accurately, efficiency is a collection of hundreds of minor choices about how we behave from day to day. Efficiency depends on a moment-to-moment conscious evolution in our behavior concerning time.

Now that I'm older, I can really appreciate the things my mother did when I was a child to help me show up at school. Despite the energy of youth, the demands of my many chores and schoolwork made me slow to stir in the morning. I hid under the covers, imagining that I could somehow steal time from the day and still get to school. It was a recipe for disaster. Left to my own devices, I would have arrived at lunchtime—if at all!

With an eye toward teaching me something about success, my mother played lively music every morning to help me wake up. At breakfast, she talked to me about how much fun I would have at school that day. She reminded me how well-prepared I was, pointing out that I had completed my homework the night before. Somehow, she always worked the miracle of getting me out the door on time. I arrived at school confident and ready.

When I moved away from home to go to college, my confidence stayed strong, but my punctuality and self-discipline suffered. At first I was late for almost every class and put off all my homework assignments until the last minute. Needless to say, this lack of time management was reflected in my grades. My imperfect grades made me miserable, and my misery tempted me more and more to hide under the covers and avoid starting a new day. However, in our mistakes we can find our breakthroughs. At the beginning of my sophomore year, I realized I had to take charge. I bought a day planner and began an ongoing quest to make the most of my time.

Time Management

Time management tools are well worth acquiring and mastering. They are central to challenging old habits and testing new reactions. As an aspect of personal mastery, time management has a big impact on our ability to get a handle on the interpersonal realm.

Time management is a great way to test how we're putting our values into practice with other people. We are proving ourselves, to ourselves and to others. The better we manage our time, the better we can manage all our other resources. We improve our habits by making new choices about one single sheet of paper, one e-mail, or one phone call at a time.

As leaders, we're constantly modeling how to manage time. Our success or failure in this endeavor determines how productive everyone around us can be. The people on the other side of our choices about time will have more of us or less. They will have our full attention or not. They will react by emulation or frustration. Worst of all, we can undermine the freedom of others to manage their own time if our poor habits impose on their schedules. When leaders are inefficient, the efficiency of the team is compromised.

Treating time as a precious commodity is a value we either put into action or not. The leader's time management skills have a far-reaching collateral impact. By consciously respecting the use of time in a group, we are treating those around us as the precious resources they are. Time management in leadership is about respect for others, freeing them to live and work respectfully of everyone from colleagues to clients, customers and other constituencies.

Managing time promotes the values and vision of leadership. It puts into action our stated commitment to ensure that there is enough time, for example, to frame the right questions and get good answers, to walk around and listen, and to be open to new ideas. Time management ensures accessibility, enabling the leader to walk the talk. Walking around takes time, communication takes time, and listening takes time. Personal mastery takes time. Without an adequate amount of time, even the best conceived plans fall into disarray.

Procrastination

No time management technique will work if we continually put things off. That's why procrastination is a bad habit—and a clear sign that our time is not being managed well. Maximum output requires productive routine and regular work patterns. Procrastination creates, at best, erratic output, which in turn creates a series of crises that people must weather.

There is an argument that asserts that many talented people do their best work under pressure. In a sense, that's true. There are many junctures in the current global market when everyone has to step up to the plate and work at top speed and under intense pressure. This is part of the fierce competition in global markets and regional economies. The problem occurs when the exception becomes the habit, and the habit becomes the culture.

It's true that living close to the edge can improve, rather than diminish, quality. But a culture that works on adrenaline cannot sustain long-term, dependable results. The habit of disruption reduces the time available to explore new information and cultivate productive working relationships. These are key ingredients in a culture of transformation.

Procrastination and crisis drain resources—not just for the person who delays her work until the last minute, but for all the other work and colleagues whose schedules and goals depend on her late results. When workflow is regularly disrupted in this way, the organization will be just as regularly rattled by the crisis du jour.

Ultimately, the crisis mentality is a force for inequality, because in crisis mode one person's priorities usually trump those of all other persons. The crisis-maker becomes dominant in a group dynamic in which each person should be able to find support for individual successes. It's not uncommon for a person to create unnecessary crises for personal reasons. An entire working culture can be hijacked by one person's bad habits or unresolved issues.

One antidote to the habit of crisis is to offer explanations that stress the importance of people's schedules and offer good reasons for overriding everyone's priorities. An explanation can put an end to the crisis. In other words, communication is the remedy, and communicating a meaningful vision gives meaning to a difficult request being made.

The solution to procrastination is time management. Unless we specifically set aside blocks of time for certain tasks in our schedules, the tasks are unlikely to get done on time—or at all. As we become conscious of our bad habits, we can practice new reactions to tasks that seem easily put off. We can choose to set deadlines for ourselves and make sure that unfinished tasks do not begin to clutter our work lives.

Procrastination is a common bad habit, and new ways of responding to the environment in a more efficient way do not come easily for most people. But it's possible to imagine a way to break through. Prepare yourself mentally by visualizing what working on the project will feel like. Collect the materials you'll need and choose a good place to work. Then just start working. Take one step, any step.

Just get moving. Once you're engaged, be sure to take breaks. Exhaustion is an experience of defeat. When it's time to return to the task, the same routines will work again. Remember, as leaders we're living examples to others about how to contribute to our shared goals.

Clutter is a manifestation of procrastination. Each piece of paper or unanswered phone message represents a choice to put off a decision.

Tasks can clutter our consciousness. They belong on To Do lists, which carry the burden of keeping track of priorities and all aspects of tasks. The list leaves our brains free to solve problems, and to communicate and listen. Of course, a To Do list can be cluttered, too. Lists that sort by priority and organize work into realistic subsets enable us to put our values into action. Scheduling time to walk around and listen, and to regroup quietly alone, shows that you're progressing in your ability to manage time and master interpersonal interactions.

Paper and e-mail clutter can be quicksand for effectiveness. Clarity and vision are hard to communicate from behind a mountain of paper, and productivity is hard to promote when e-mails back up in your inbox. Mess communicates an inability to make decisions, because every piece of paper on top of a desk is a decision we have failed to make. Despite what some people believe, a cluttered desk does not indicate genius. It can signal confusion and create stress. Practicing new ways to deal with paper involves making a commitment to touch each document only once, get it to the right place by responding in real time, and file consciously.

Telephone calls are probably the tasks that are easiest to postpone. And yet, telephone calls are important modes of communication and methods of making connections and exercising interpersonal mastery. Procrastinating about telephone calls is procrastinating about leading.

There are some tricks of the trade to help us practice new reactions to making and returning telephone calls. Batching calls and returning them in a block reduces disruption. Prepare for calls by deciding in advance how much time each call warrants and defining what needs to be said. The process of personal mastery takes this effort deeper. Sometimes putting off telephone calls is about resistance or avoidance toward a person or a responsibility. Admitting this to ourselves is the first step in overcoming it, so that we, as leaders, can remain in motion.

In a culture of transformation, leaders are people in motion. They are flexible and open, because they are constantly ready to challenge themselves. They are vigilant, because they've chosen to evolve consciously. For everyone, including leaders, procrastination is about being stalled. Clutter is about being mired. Procrastination and clutter are signs of leaders who are not in motion and cultures that are not skilled in transformation.

CHAPTER EIGHT

Interpersonal Mastery

Small Gestures and Great Leaps Forward

Interpersonal mastery is the second of the three types of expertise needed for success in leading an organization, and it's the type that most people associate with leaders. It evolves out of our personal mastery work and comprises a set of skills that can be learned by anyone who is willing to make the commitment and put forth the effort. Like personal mastery, it is reflected in the cumulative power of small gestures and courtesies.

Much has been written about the critical importance of social skills to leadership. John T. Molloy said that while he was researching his book (*Molloy's Live for Success*), 99 out of every 100 executives he surveyed said that social skills were a prerequisite for success in business and in life.[22] There is common agreement, as well, that business is all about relationships. Mastering skills for productive interpersonal exchanges and group dynamics is essential for leaders.

The very important tactics involved in "people skills" deserve much attention; at TSI we work extensively with leaders and groups to promote interpersonal mastery. What we return to, again and again, is how personal mastery is at the core of interpersonal skills. At the risk of repeating myself about a central factor in leadership success, personal mastery challenges the old attitudes, choices and habits that have hindered the development of our social abilities. Personal mastery challenges us to test new reactions in everyday life. Personal mastery removes barriers to interpersonal successes. Interpersonal mastery relies on how well we master ourselves; it challenges us to understand that successful interactions with others involve awareness of cues and of other people's needs, and a willingness to listen to what they have to say.

Personal mastery continues indefinitely. With each new season and new set of goals, we are pushed to grow anew before we can energize those around us to do the same. The principles of personal mastery remain constant. As a way of life, it is the right order of things. We confront ourselves with growth before we go out and lead others into challenges that stretch them. Walking the talk makes us credible and authentic.

The more we master ourselves, the freer we are to become catalysts for productive exchanges and dynamics. Conscious evolution frees us to recognize and volunteer to be the type of leader the group needs at any given moment. We have become flexible and open, because we're no longer tottering with the imbalance cause by old attitudes, choices or habits. We're open to new attitudes, new choices and new habits in our lives.

In the culture of transformation, every contributor has full permission to participate fully. The leader who is experienced with personal mastery can step in and play any number of roles, including guide, facilitator, motivator or catalyst. Without personal mastery as a way of life, we're less adaptable and less willing to evolve into the role that's needed at the moment. The better we know ourselves, the more we can be. With personal mastery, we can be many things to different people in various settings, while remaining constant in our vision and intention.

No matter what role we're playing, we must be mindful that a variety of tasks, talents and personalities are at work. Leadership integrates. It unifies. As leaders, we manage the power of others to welcome dynamic creativity while fostering balance in the group. We model respect for diversity of opinion and style, encouraging range and openness among all participants. This attitude ensures that cooperation replaces competition. We lead in the etiquette we practice with others as we shepherd all the best talent toward a shared goal.

This is how leaders transform the chaos of creativity into unity. They create balance within creative diversity. In unity, the group becomes productive and enjoys shared achievement. The organization operates with unrivaled capacity, and it competes readily in the demanding new world reality.

All this can happen when leaders choose to be in motion and stay in motion.

The ongoing process of personal mastery inspires clarity, renews commitment, and expands energy. The motion from detachment to interaction (and back again) is constant and fluid. We emerge from solitude into the collective hubbub of the group's effort. This can happen in a matter of moments, or after a weekend spent reflecting, or during workshops and meetings. What matters is that the leader has been able to harness the power found in the solitude of leadership. He can now move fluidly between the realms of detachment and interaction, from personal mastery to interpersonal mastery and back again.

The impact of this process is great. Our conscious evolution weeds out old attitudes, choices and habits. We challenge ourselves to practice whole new reactions. Barriers to relationships at all levels disappear. We are changing. We are committed to changing and growing. We continue to transform. We become the catalysts for a culture of transformation.

Managing Image

What leaders say communicates vision, and what they do helps others visualize new directions and great success. This is as true of the detail as of the broad stroke. For instance, leaders set examples of respect for work and for others. We either project self-care, or we don't, which is why leaders must manage their own stress and do their best to look good. Our choices about appearance and about how we manage the impression we make reflect our ability to respect ourselves—and others. While appearance is created in the detail of how we present ourselves visually, it creates a vision of the success and confidence we have in our minds.

The first reaction many clients have to suggestions about looking great is to focus on one or two negative points about themselves. But personal mastery resists that impulse. Making strides to look and sound fabulous can energize others. We begin by accepting who we are—our strengths and weaknesses—and then do the best with everything we have. Professional success is not a beauty contest, but for leaders it's a test of how much we can inspire trust and creativity in others. It pays to express creativity in our image.

In a way, we can see interpersonal mastery as beginning with first impressions, and first impressions rely on how we look and sound. Lasting impressions rely on the same things. How we sit and stand can project confidence in the midst of challenge—or drain energy from a meeting. Clothing, hair, accessories and shoes are part of our package. How we choose to appear expresses self-care or disregard. If we have little regard for ourselves, we're unlikely to earn the trust of others. The words we choose can amplify—or undermine—the visual image of clarity, commitment and energy we project.

An impeccable image is about feeling great and leading consciously.

Protocol

Guidelines—even rules—exist for interpersonal mastery. Many companies have established rules of protocol as part of their culture to ensure smooth daily operations and provide a competitive advantage. These are important to understand. But circumstances change, and business activities are affected by new settings. In a culture of transformation, these unwritten rules frequently need to evolve along with people. Conscious awareness means we neither dismiss the unwritten rules around us nor blindly follow them. We exercise judgment. We take the lead in how we deal with colleagues.

Certain habits of etiquette do not change with circumstances or new settings. They tend to work in any setting. "Etiquette" may sound like an outdated word. For my ninth birthday, I received a set of books from my parents. It was a series known as *The Random House Hostess Library*. It included an etiquette manual. Along with the gift, my mother offered a bit of advice: "Marta, you must learn good manners. Using them is never your choice; it's your responsibility."

My mother was right. Basic manners never expire, and the need for them never changes. They've been crucial to my success in business and to my own personal mastery. They make us memorable, and they're worth remembering. Good manners are at the core of business etiquette, and they can be leveraged into ever more productive relationships. Practicing them is a key step toward interpersonal mastery.

We need to know how to dine with good manners, how to carry on polite conversation, how to introduce people without falling all over ourselves, and how to comply with simple rules of courtesy. Keeping an eye on our small courtesies is an important means of self-challenge.

One guiding principle is to remember that small things matter. Nowhere is this principle more true and powerful than in the world of business, where niceties and social amenities can mean the difference between simply getting by and gaining the edge necessary to excel in today's fiercely competitive environment.

Many people don't understand exactly how much little things count until they ignore them and suffer the consequences—everything from embarrassment to reassignment to job loss. It's no exaggeration to say that business protocol can influence our success dramatically. Being courteous, polite and pleasant is the mark of a leader who has chosen to interact with others consciously—alert to their talents and needs, and prepared to serve. Business etiquette lies at the heart of business relationships, which lie at the heart of business success. Good etiquette is an exercise in smart heart .. but more on that a little later.

Casual Interactions

Practicing new reactions in casual conversation is a natural step to advance interpersonal mastery. If we want to be able to wander around and listen, we must be easy to meet and greet. Our body language must reflect approachability. We smile, make eye contact generously, use names, and project a positive and friendly attitude in every interaction. Our goodwill does not discriminate. Everyone is worth meeting, if only momentarily. Those momentary interactions can leave lasting impressions, and we never know when our paths will cross again.

Mingling is a skill most people connect with office holiday parties, but it's important any time we walk into a room. Pausing at the entrance and surveying the room gives us time to see who's there and who we need to talk to. A willingness to remain mobile, moving around the room, never staying with one person too long, lets us connect in a small way with most people. Small talk is the key to initiating new relationships and maintaining old ones. Making comfortable small talk relies on a conscious decision to prepare each day to talk about news or sports or other matters, so that what you say allows everyone to participate. Small talk—the talk of mingling—is inclusive. Mingling is literally a leader in motion.

Whether in meetings or on the street outside the office, introducing people can open whole new business directions—and not introducing them can result in lost opportunities. A common habit is to treat time outside the office or in the halls as private time, and sometimes it may need to be. But almost anywhere we go can be an opportunity to meet and greet people. Introductions are an art form. The right body language and the correct business etiquette for introducing people are skills we can learn as we develop interpersonal mastery. Remembering names is important, but it's possible to be charmingly honest about forgetting a name. We can learn specific ways to help keep a conversation going. Compliments should be pleasant comments on skills or achievements, not awkward references to appearance. Introductions begin and extend our very important network. Interpersonal mastery makes them an art form.

Helping is a commendable impulse among colleagues, customers and clients. Yet because of changing social mores, people are often most awkward when it comes to helping each other. Here again, personal mastery is important. Opening a door is a thoughtful gesture regardless of the genders of the people involved. Helping someone carry packages or put on a coat is not a mistake, as long as we're honest and comfortable with the way we offer and receive help.

Our conscious choices in all aspects of casual encounters—and the image we project—reflect our level of interpersonal mastery.

Heart

One way leaders develop bonds with and among the contributors around them is to foster bonds between people and ideas. That way, a vision becomes a shared goal that unifies intention and will. By engaging the heart of everyone in important transformational goals, leaders prepare groups to share accomplishment, which would not be possible if all or most of them were not motivated by a heart connection to the vision.

Interpersonal mastery is also a process of caring about people, and caring about people leads to a certain ease about being a colleague, a helper, a mentor—and a leader. Mastery in matters of the heart goes far beyond business etiquette, although good manners let people know that their feelings will be respected. Mastery of social skills also goes beyond motivating people to let their hearts be captivated by good ideas. Interpersonal mastery is about "heart smarts."

Leaders need to understand how much their work accomplishments rely on the heart, and they need to honor the heart. This understanding permits us to lead from the heart and enables us to capture the hearts and minds of people who will make their best contributions when they're more than just employed—when they're inspired and fully engaged. Until change occurs in the hearts around us, the workplace cannot transform, and we cannot achieve authentic or sustainable progress. Leaders integrate heart with vision and intention. Transformation must happen in the heart as well as in habits, or change will be superficial and old habits will slip back into place when the pressure is high—just when a new and better way of working is most important.

James MacDonald, regional vice president of human resources, Eastern Region, for Hilton Hotels Corporation, tells a story about how the heart can initiate and sustain authentic transformation in a culture. He shared this story with me during a conversation in the company's New York offices.

In the early 1990s, when Doubletree was still a small chain of hotels, management decided to launch a company-wide initiative to radically change the culture. The initiative was the CARE (Caring and Responsive Employee) program. CARE sought to evaluate and transform the leadership, employees and daily processes. Jim was charged with rolling CARE out to all employees.

As appealing as the vision for transformation was, Jim and the HR directors were unable to overcome the general employee resistance to a management dictate that had no heart. People needed to transform the culture through their daily choices, but their hearts had not been captured. Jim decided to take a different approach, to appeal to what he called the "unseen" leaders.

He started by seeking to capture the heart of one man—a man he knew appreciated the idea behind CARE. He took the man and his wife out to dinner to talk about the program. They talked about the man's leadership qualities and the impact he could have on the company through CARE. They talked about how the initiative would affect the welfare of employees' families. The next day, Jim asked the general manager to talk to the man about the need for his leadership contribution. Jim also asked the man's direct supervisor to free up some of his time so he could work on CARE. After all the barriers to his commitment had been removed, the man agreed to officially assume the leadership role for the program. Immediately, 25 people joined the committee charged with infusing the corporation with CARE. About 80 percent of the committee members were hourly workers, and the other 20 percent were first- and second-level managers. Jim stayed on as a consultant to what had become a forum for working people implementing CARE. Soon, being on the committee was considered a plum position, and people had to apply. Jim had managed to capture the hearts of the people who could make the necessary changes.

The committee focused on both employee and customer programs, determining what promoted satisfaction in each and ensuring that the best programs were retained. From the start, the committee had a strong foundation, purpose and goal. Some committee members gravitated naturally to customer relations, others to employee relations. The CARE committee grew strong with the commitment and energy of its members, and it evolved to the point where it governed itself. Leadership on the committee began to lead to career advancement in the organization. The CARE committee was capturing the imagination of the entire workforce and was finding and developing new leaders.

The committee members enjoyed the support of senior management and were free to do what they wanted. They developed policy and implemented new ideas across the company, in all the hotels. The committee developed the idea of CARE Buddies, who took new employees out to lunch on their first day and introduced them around the hotel to other employees. CARE Buddies even took the new employees on a tour of New York City, reasoning that they had to know the city to properly welcome guests to the city. The committee initiated peer interviews for job candidates, and it planned all staff celebrations and holiday parties. A massive safety review was experienced by workers, not as management trying to spare itself a multimillion-dollar lawsuit but as colleagues trying to improve everyone's safety. Today, a version of the CARE program is in place throughout the Hilton chain; it has a particularly strong impact on the culturally diversified workforce in the industry.

Employee relations were energized. Jim's role remained one of guidance and direction, but the CARE committee evolved to the point that all staff saw it as their voice and influence on the company and on their own work lives. It was viewed as a positive force, so admired by the staff that, when Hilton took over Doubletree, the staff voted against joining the union. They already felt powerful and listened to because of the CARE committee. Management actually found itself encouraging the workers to join the union!

Results in guest relations were similarly stunning. The Doubletree hotel at which the original CARE committee was formed under Jim's guidance stayed in the top 10 of all the company's properties, because guests felt the happiness and energy of the staff. Guest loyalty scores increased in response to the growth of the CARE culture. So did repeat business scores and the willingness of guests to complete the rating or comment card in the first place. Guests feel the commitment. That can't be faked. It's from the heart.

Building Bonds

Interpersonal mastery is about personal mastery expanding outward, naturally. It involves conscious changes in habits and attitudes when dealing with others, and it includes an ability to communicate new ideas in such a way that ideas can connect with and inspire the hearts of everyone who is expected to contribute to an outcome. Strong bonds are great avenues to relay energy, vision and impact.

Interpersonal mastery is also about building bonds.

When we build bonds, we create and sustain relationships. All our institutions are relationship-based: organizations, government, business, sports teams, marriages. Bonds can be created easily, but it takes work to sustain them. Relationships must be sparked, nurtured, managed, created and recreated. They require clear expectations, commitment and energy. They require time.

Some people seem to be born relationship-builders. Most of us, however, must work at relationships. But whether through natural talent or effort, or even through sheer will power, anyone can achieve mastery at building relationships. That's because leadership is possible for everyone and, in relationships, at one time or another everyone must take the lead.

Good relationship skills include awareness of others' feelings, needs and concerns. That's the only way to win hearts and to work from the heart. Relationships rely on three factors: building bonds, communication and influencing others.

Bonds free us to know each other in ways that can overcome mountains of personal differences and hard feelings. Alliances create power. President Abraham Lincoln's famous statement gets to the heart of the matter: "A house divided against itself cannot stand." Leaders seek to build unity in small and large, formal and informal relationships. Relationships working in unity are very strong—and very creative. Relationships between people who do not exercise interpersonal mastery suffer and falter.

Bonds enable us to relay cutting-edge reality checks. Hugh Gouldthorpe, Jr., senior vice president of quality and communications at Owens & Minor, cites Sam Walton's book, *Made in America: My Story,* and its 10 rules for running a successful company. Walton's

Rule #4 focuses on "communicating everything you can to your asso-ciates, teammates, and customers. The more people know and understand, the more they care. Once they care, there's no stopping them."[23]

Hugh told me that in the 1980s and 1990s, he was determined to get the most authentic feedback possible to create the Owens & Minor vision and mission statements. After many efforts to do this without input from outside stakeholders, he decided to include them in the process. He said, "Don't try to guess what the customer wants. Go and sit with them. Ask them what we are doing right and what can we do to improve and serve you better. In that way, you get defin-itive input that you can use to improve your organization."

Bonds are the building blocks of success.

Communication

Communication is the keystone in building bonds. Done right, it can deepen relationships and expand our reach through maturing net-works of relationships.

Communications competence clearly distinguishes stars from average and poor performers—and leaders from managers. Good communicators are effective in give-and-take. They hone their ability to sense others' emotions so they can fine-tune their own messages. They deal with difficult issues straightforwardly. They listen well and seek mutual understanding. Adept communicators foster open dia-logue and are receptive to bad news as well as good. Communication permits the relay of all the best a group has to offer, but also of infor-mation about obstacles and problems. Managing communication involves managing what is relayed within an organization—motiva-tion and transformation or fear and hesitation.

Casual contact is as important as formal gatherings for building bonds and maintaining networks. The more we cultivate a setting in which people are able to relax and be open about their thoughts and feelings, the stronger are the foundations of our bonds. Creating an atmosphere of openness is not a trivial gesture. The biggest single complaint of American workers is poor communication with co-workers; most even say it prevents them from doing their best work.[24]

The basics of communication seem simple enough, as long as we remember that we communicate in many different ways and that the manner in which we communicate with others almost always determines how they will communicate back to us. If we concentrate on improving the quality of our communication, people will be more likely to understand us. This connection enhances and improves our ability to work together in accomplishing the goals that are most important to us.

Not every leader must rival Winston Churchill's artful rhetoric, although we can learn from his personal discipline and the communication skills he practiced. In particular, his ability to listen and his openness to other people's ideas are lessons for all of us. Communication genius is marked by effective listening. Listening has many forms. We ask astute questions. We consciously choose to be open-minded and to try to understand. We do not interrupt. We ask for and welcome suggestions. The voices of colleagues, mentors and customers all matter and warrant our attention. Most important, until we master our resistance to hearing what others think, feel and need, we cannot listen, no matter how many books on communication we read or seminars we attend. Listening is among the most frequently taught business skills, and possibly the skill least likely to be mastered.

Persuasion

Persuasion is a particular type of communication that deserves a special place in a book for leaders. Unless the business model is a dictatorship, persuasion is second only to speaking in the list of basic skills a leader must master. As long as our efforts to persuade are heartfelt and based on strong bonds of respect, persuasion does not become manipulation.

Abraham Lincoln was a great persuader—a leader with heroic values at a watershed moment in history. Biographies consistently portray him as a man who influenced people with his friendly manner, openness and verbal skills. In 1836, at the age of 27 and during his second term in the Illinois legislature, Lincoln created a plan to move the capital of the state from Vandalia to Springfield. Clever bargaining, coupled with persistence and persuasiveness, enabled him to overcome what was thought to be insurmountable resistance and pull off a political coup. Later in his life, Lincoln worked with generals who did not have to obey his commands at all times, and yet, throughout the war, his letters show him persuading them to his point of view.[25]

Lincoln's own view of the importance of persuasion is renowned. In 1843, he offered these historic remarks to the Springfield, Illinois, Washingtonian Temperance Society: "When the conduct of men is designed to be influenced, persuasion—kind, unassuming persuasion—should ever be adopted. It is an old and a true maxim that a drop of honey catches more flies than a gallon of gall."[26]

Persuasion is not directive. We persuade by suggestion—and by exercising patience while people make their own decisions on the basis of full information. That's why taking the time to establish a bond is not a detour but an essential step in influencing others. In a study of strategic decisions at 356 American companies, more than half were never adopted, were implemented only partially, or were abandoned at the outset. The single most common reason identified for the failure of these plans was that the lead executives tried to impose their ideas instead of building a supporting consensus. When ideas were dictated, the result was failure 58 percent of the time. But when executives first conferred with colleagues to rethink their long-term priorities, strategic plans were adopted 96 percent of the time.

Reaching into the heart of the listener and seeing things from his or her point of view is crucial for persuasion. Listening is only a start. Being aware of the intentions and emotions of others is crucial for wielding influence. It's difficult to have a positive impact on others without first sensing how they feel and understanding their position. People who are poor at reading emotional cues and inept at social interactions are very bad at influencing others. People who are good at influencing others fine-tune their presentations to appeal to the listener. They orchestrate dramatic events to make a point that will resonate with their particular audience. People adept at influence can sense or anticipate their audience's reaction to their message.

This requires vigilance and conscious flexibility. We need to respond in real time to feedback. When logical arguments are falling flat, we can move to appeals that are more to the heart. We must exercise social competence. Real-time response strategies used by top performers include impression management, appeals to reason and facts, and well-placed dramatic actions. If we want to be able to respond effectively to the people in our working environment, we need to cultivate an awareness of others and what is important to them.

Networks

Relationships are the core of our networks. New and maturing bonds expand those networks. Studies of outstanding performers in engineering, computer science, biotechnology and other "knowledge work" fields find that building and maintaining personal networks is crucial for success. People who are competent at building bonds naturally cultivate and maintain extensive informal networks. They seek out relationships that are mutually beneficial, and then they build rapport. They develop personal friendships among their work associates. This talent for connecting characterizes stars in almost every kind of job.

A spirit of generosity deepens our network connections. Many people are too protective of their own time and agenda, and turn down requests to help or work cooperatively with others. The result is resentment and a stunted network. On the other hand, people who can't say no are in danger of taking on so much that their own effectiveness suffers. Again, resentment is the result. Outstanding performers are able to balance their own critical work with carefully chosen favors, building accounts of goodwill with people who may be crucial resources down the line.

Networks include both courtesy and trust; and strong bonds, whether personal or professional, require both. Trust is the essential building block for successful relationships. The more mutual trust we have with another person, the more honest and productive the relationship can become. In fact, one of the virtues of building networks is the reservoir of goodwill and trust that arises. This is particularly crucial for advancement from the lower rungs of an organization to the higher levels. These human links are the routes through which people come to be known for their abilities. Networks built on trust can be the most supportive alliances in our efforts to lead groups to greatness.

In creating alliances, Lincoln was uniquely adept at interpersonal mastery. The first impression might be that his ability was innate, but history tells us that he worked at those skills to advance his goals in the midst of national turmoil. He was faced with limits on how much he could force any of his subordinates to do, but he went beyond those limits by persuading people to share his vision. His intention was constant, along with his vision that disparate opinions among powerful leaders could be integrated into a unified nation.

Differences are part of relationships, so managing networks and alliances as they mature requires skillful management of differences. Lincoln stands out as a leader who managed differences. One of the most striking things he did was to help those around him make decisions without his constant supervision. As he built strong bonds with others, he was taking the time to learn how they would respond in various situations—and encouraging them to learn the same about him. If others knew what he would do, and he knew what they would do, he could trust their judgment and they could rely on him for support. He trusted people to contribute as leaders themselves.

There are many advantages to having well-developed networks. People who use their networks judiciously have an immense time advantage over those who have to use broader, more general sources of information to find answers. It's estimated that for every hour a well-connected individual spends seeking answers through a network, the average person would spend three to five hours gathering the same information. A network can also help a person influence others—the network's endorsement creates added support and credibility for an idea.

A network of contacts is crucial personal capital. It is an example of the fruits of interpersonal mastery returning for personal, individual benefit. Among leaders, what benefits the individual also benefits the group. So the network of contacts we bring to the job is, in fact, a wealth of knowledge, support and goodwill we bring to everyone around us. If we're building good bonds throughout our careers, we're building a leadership network full of people outside our daily circles who can contribute richly to the goals to which our group aspires.

Top performers do not create random networks. A network can be an exercise in choice. Each person is included because of a particular expertise or excellence. These networks send information back and forth in an artful, ongoing give-and-take. Each member of a network represents an immediately available extension of knowledge, accessible with a single phone call. While physical proximity helps, it's psychological proximity that cements these connections. Successful networks are not happenstance. Selecting participants requires awareness about what each might contribute, including not just expertise but optimism; not just the ability to critique, but the ability to encourage. For a leader, the network can be an alternative source of support when the isolation of a position or a circumstance may leave us with few trusted confidantes.

Teamwork

Networks are not the same as teams, although we often find that working in teams creates new connections that expand our networks. Never underestimate the value of a team experience, even after the team is disbanded. Teams are central to transformation and achievement.

"Ain't none of us as good as all of us." Hugh Gouldthorpe provided me with an example of this adage. He told me that sometimes, when he visits the company's distribution centers, he gives everyone a sheet of paper with a heading that reads, "The ABCs of Teamwork," with 25 C's going down the left side of the page. He asks each person to come up with as many characteristics of good teamwork as possible that start with the letter C. The most any one person usually gets in three to five minutes is 15 to 17 words. In a group of 30 people, he divides them into six teams and asks them to come up with as many words as possible. In three to five minutes, the list of 17 becomes 30. Next he combines the group into three teams of 10 each, and finally into one team of 30. During the process, the list increases to more than 200 words. Hugh's point is that no one can think of everything and come up with all the answers. Individuals don't win; teams do.

Meetings

Meetings are one way teams interact in a more formal setting. They provide excellent opportunities to exchange ideas, clarify issues, resolve concerns, communicate consistently to a group, and involve groups in decisions. Meetings can be used to relay almost any facet of an organization's need or activities. At their best, they can even be networks in action. The success of a meeting rests on the ability to cultivate psychological proximity and advance the goals of all the members. The topic of a meeting warrants careful reflection from every angle.

In meetings, all our interpersonal skills come into play—and we can evolve to new levels of competence. Meetings consume much of the average professional worker's time. Too often, they paralyze an organization, sapping the time and energy of all concerned. In some corporate cultures, meetings have become an entrenched habit and, like any habit, are so routine that they no longer are measured against original intention. The result is that too many talented people are stuck in a marathon, running from meeting room to meeting room, focused everywhere but on the actual business of doing business.

When a group gathers for a meeting, there is great potential for contributing to success, so meetings play a central role in the life of any organization. But every business can benefit from honestly evaluating its use of meetings, to make sure they are valuable tools. With a few guidelines and some conscious effort, group goals can be matched to meeting goals. Then we just need to take responsibility for managing the details around and during the meeting.

Perhaps the most important thing to know about meetings is when *not* to meet. How a culture is run by meetings is a telling sign of how well time—a precious resource—is respected in the group and managed by individuals. Meetings are not needed to discuss trivial subjects or to disseminate information that could be distributed using other means. When a leader's mind is made up, a meeting is an empty gesture, stealing time from other work and undermining the progress of work outside the meeting. Meetings should not occur without adequate data and good preparation. Most important, when the group dynamic is intensely emotional—for example, full of anger—productivity will be impossible until the conflict is resolved.

The use of effective ground rules is the most powerful tool for managing a meeting. In workshops based on TSI's *Transformation Desktop Guide* and *Live a Difference,* we recommend a few never-fail rules. Some of them are described below. It's important that ground rules are communicated directly. The best approach is an open discussion that seeks the commitment of all participants before proceeding. What does *not* work is simply posting the rules or distributing them on paper.

Preparing for a meeting is crucial, because meeting time must be wisely used. When there is a reason to hold a meeting, the first step is to decide on the purpose of the meeting. As Steven Covey says, begin with the end in mind. Defining the kind of meeting you need to achieve a clear goal gives purpose to the gathering. Some meetings are about sharing information and status updates; others are about problem solving and decision making; and others are about learning and development. Most meetings build teams; they all build bonds.

Time spent shaping a meeting in advance is time well used. Almost every meeting can benefit from a comprehensive and well-thought-through agenda. Mapping various aspects of an agenda can ensure the best results. Define what needs to be accomplished in the meeting and after the meeting. Break the meeting into modules or time segments, each with a clear goal and process. If necessary, rely on a timer to keep things moving. Meetings, like leaders, need to be kept in motion. Pacing keeps contributors at their best energy level.

The meeting opening can make the difference between success and failure. An opening can be formal and detailed or informal and brief, but it sets tone and expectations quickly, offering a welcome and the necessary introductions. A review of the ground rules, roles and expectations for outputs and outcomes helps focus the group. Describing the agenda items lets participants know what to expect and how they can contribute. The opening helps free members to contribute their best.

Meetings can be grueling. Keeping the energy level up requires planning and a willingness to respond to regular reads of the group.

Vary the medium. Break into smaller groups. Use energizers. Manage the temperature. Use a U-shaped setup if possible, because people around the edge of a room are energy leaks. Each person's energy level influences everyone else in the room, so participants need to manage their own energy for the good of the group. Ask them directly to do so. (For example, sitting slumped over can cut off 30 percent of the oxygen to the brain.)

Consensus is often the best type of decision making for group process. A consensus is a decision made by the group that all members may not entirely agree with but can support completely. Consensus contributes to community buy-in. Majority voting is most effective when the group has a long list of options that must be narrowed down to a smaller, more manageable list. Voting should not be used to make a final decision on the one best option; it creates a minority of potentially disgruntled participants.

The leader's sensitivity and flexibility help foster respect, protect individuals from personal attacks, and encourage a climate of acceptance and patience. These traits are needed in the facilitator of the meeting, and in official and unofficial leaders as well. Tact is one way to be sensitive and flexible about other people's needs; it requires the ability to think before speaking.

The facilitator monitors and maintains the level of participation, contribution and energy in a meeting. He or she is in charge of the process; that is, how the group works together. The facilitator should be process-oriented, which includes developing the meeting outcome and agenda, choosing methods (such as brainstorming), and pointing out ways the group can work together more effectively.

Facilitators

Most organizations are concerned with improving performance. Generally, they can motivate employees by giving groups the authority to do what they think is best. The organization benefits because a group of people working together to make the best possible decisions is generally better than one person directing others. When groups are truly involved, they're more willing to give their wholehearted support, because they own their decisions and will strive to implement them successfully. Meetings are most often the setting for groups to exercise their power.

Facilitators make or break a meeting. If the facilitator has worked with the group before, he arrives in the room with rapport already in place, because he has already helped the group—both during and after meetings—make decisions, develop plans, and implement actions that lead to desired results. A good facilitator must simultaneously manage time, energy and results. The facilitator's success is largely determined by how well he can manage the seemingly small courtesies needed for good business and the seemingly tiny gestures needed for positive connections.

Groups need objectivity. They count on the facilitator to take a bird's eye view of the meeting, so participants can concentrate on voicing ideas, making decisions, and achieving results. The facilitator must keep the discussion going, monitor what's happening, and structure the group's approach. Skilled facilitation bolsters the group's energy and commitment.

Leaders often do not facilitate their own meetings. Instead, they rely on a facilitator who is content-neutral, which means she does not share personal opinions but, rather, helps the group confer and decide. For group members to have the authority to make a decision themselves, they must not face a facilitator who forces her opinion on them. If the decision-making exercise is a sham and the participants are disempowered in practice, they will withdraw and simply stop participating. By keeping the meeting on course and at a productive level, the facilitator represents the commitment of leadership to those whose contributions they need.

The best meeting facilitator is the person who can be authentically neutral on the issues being discussed. As she guides the group and keeps them organized, the facilitator must allow participants to make their own decisions. The group must take ownership for the business issues being addressed. By focusing on process and remaining content-neutral, the facilitator helps the group members use their skills and experience to achieve their intended results. It's important not to judge or criticize others during a meeting. If the group is off-topic, the facilitator can point out how they are using their energy.

Meeting facilitators demonstrate tactfulness by thinking before they speak and by expressing their thoughts clearly but with humility. The facilitator must be assertive but tactful in enforcing the ground rules, maintaining adherence to procedures, and giving feedback and direction. The facilitator enables the participants to make good use of limited time and guides the group toward success. The facilitator is a leader in action.

A recap or summary is the last module on the agenda. The facilitator helps the group review outputs and outcomes, and any decisions made during the meeting. This recap shows that the contract to honor the participants and their time has been kept. However, the work is not finished. Follow-up may be necessary, and the results of the meeting are usually published for the participants and those who were unable to attend. The final step is a formal or informal evaluation of the meeting's effectiveness.

Inclusion and Involvement

When I talked with Hugh Gouldthorpe, Jr., senior vice president of quality and communications for Owens & Minor, he had many inspiring stories about the power of inclusion, involvement and effective teamwork in organizational success.

In addition to being a senior vice president, Hugh is also known as the head cheerleader for this Fortune 500 organization. He told me this story: "When I think of examples of how inclusion has helped make a difference in the implementation of plans, I think of Children's Hospital of Philadelphia. It's one of our largest accounts in the country. In the years that we've serviced this hospital, we've moved product from our dock in New Jersey to their dock. At a certain point, we decided that we would talk with them about outsourcing the hospital's central supply to help improve their efficiency. They agreed, and we assumed responsibility for this function, which was new for everyone, as they'd always employed their own people in central supply. It was paramount that we be efficient, run the operation effectively and, most important, gain the trust of the hospital staff. To do this involved communication at all levels of the organization."

Hugh is a big believer in the role of inclusion and involvement in the path to success. "You must include and involve people. In our company, every teammate and customer is an important stakeholder. The key, I feel, is giving people the freedom to express themselves. At Owens & Minor, people feel they can walk in and say, 'Hugh, this is what we need to do to get better.' When people ask me how many customer service reps we have, I say 4,525. Folks are often shocked by this number until they discover we also have 4,525 teammates. Everyone in the company is a customer service representative in some capacity."

In his leadership book *I've Always Looked Up to Giraffes,* Hugh explained that giraffes have a lot to teach us about the best ways to involve and include the right stakeholders. The giraffe is not the strongest or the fastest animal; however, it is the friendliest animal in the animal kingdom. It understands power—how and when to use it, and when and where to guide others. That knowledge makes it the most powerful and respected animal by far.

Hugh recalled how, in the late 1980s and early 1990s, Owens & Minor was working on its mission and vision statements. "We were struggling like mad, so we decided to go to the people who worked with us. We talked to them to see what they thought our mission and vision should be. We sat with general managers running distribution centers and teammates across the nation working in our warehouses to get the information from them." They acted with the wisdom of giraffes.

At one point, Hugh was attending a program conducted by Ken Blanchard, in which they were discussing the idea of teamwork. He said Blanchard gave the following example: "Go home tonight, get a Ziplock bag, and fill it full of water. Seal it, then take 8 or 10 sharp pencils and stick them through the bag. Amazingly, the bag does not leak. Pull one pencil out, and the bag starts to dribble. When you pull the second pencil out, it dribbles more. And once you pull out a third, you'll have a huge puddle of water on the floor. The message is that every teammate brings something to the table to keep an organization running smoothly and to keep it from leaking." This is a wonderful illustration of the value of teamwork.

Hugh described a program that welcomed new ideas from everyone on the OM team. It reveals how much the culture of transformation is at work at Owens & Minor. He said, "We have something called Ideas Pay Off, where teammates who have ideas send them in. When the idea is received, it's acknowledged and forwarded to the appropriate team to get their input on the suggestion. The initiator is kept in the loop at all times and rewarded for bringing forth the suggestion. If the idea is accepted, the owner of the idea receives another award."

Owens & Minor goes even further in its effort to include teammates in how the company evolves. Hugh said, "It's key to get your teammates involved. As we grow, we continually move from smaller to larger facilities. In doing this, we've learned the importance of getting the right teammates involved. In the past, it might have taken 8 to 10 days to make a move. Now, with the right teammates, we can do it in a weekend." Teamwork makes the dream work. If you dream it, you can do it.

Conflict

Surveys show that in 1975 managers spent up to 30 percent of their time handling conflict; by 1996, the figure was 42 percent.[27] In today's ever-more-driven work environment, conflict is still on the rise. Some of that conflict is part of the job—like fighting to protect project resources—but a great deal of time is spent resolving interpersonal and organizational conflict. This means there's that much less energy directed toward adding value to the project or the business.

Look at the statistics on the cost of workplace violence. In addition to government oversight and control through organizations such as the Occupational Safety and Health Administration (OSHA), two organizations study the effects of workplace violence in the United States and Canada: the National Safe Workplace Institute (NSWI) and the Workplace Violence Research Institute (WVRI). It's a new area of study, and the results are amazing. Including both the direct and indirect effects of violence, the most recent WWRI statistics place the annual cost of workplace violence at $35.4 billion.[28]

Disagreements will always occur within groups, but they are rarely violent. In fact, disagreement can be healthy; for example, it can indicate growth, which is often an uncomfortable process. Disagreement can kick off a process in which colleagues educate each other and bring whole groups to new levels of awareness and honesty. Some groups can even handle unhealthy disagreements in healthy ways. For example, as group members learn to embrace their own need to pursue personal mastery and to accept informal leadership roles, individuals often work through the dynamic themselves. So, not every disagreement is a problem.

However, it's important to remain vigilant, because disagreement in a group can slow down or undermine group progress. Once disagreement takes on a life of its own, the chance that resolution will arise simply out of the group dynamic decreases, and a real conflict begins to gain a foothold. Conflict undermines a culture that seeks to be the kind of environment where transformation can unfold without impediments.

If a group cannot approach conflict in a healthy way, it may avoid it, so that the conflict becomes submerged and hard to identify. Alternatively, the group may argue excessively, getting nowhere; as the focus moves off shared goals and efforts become fragmented, the result is chaos. Groups that submerge conflict are challenging because they often don't open up. Chaotic groups are very open, but it can be hard for group members to move out of entrenched positions and reach a resolution. Sometimes the leader is too close to the dynamic to offer a detached perspective, so he is unlikely to be helpful and might even drive the conflict deeper into the group dynamic. Once conflict has taken root in a group, a facilitator is often the best way to bring the group back into the healthy range, where conflict is addressed and resolved.

Conflict is part of the workplace dynamic, but it doesn't have to be a negative drain on energy or productivity. Once we adjust our thinking and stop looking at conflict as a matter of good and bad, we can manage our conflicts and, in the process, achieve greater interpersonal and team results. Understanding some of the factors behind conflict can help us influence the dynamic for the better. One of the most important truths about conflict is that it's often not about what it seems to be about. Until we understand the real source of a conflict, we cannot successfully reduce it.

Conflict has various possible sources. Organizational conflict stems from cultural disparity, when espoused values and beliefs differ from the actual ones. This conflict is centered on the infrastructure of the organization. Organizational psychologist Julian B. Rotter developed the "locus of control" theory, which applies here. When people struggle with the extent to which they are able to control their own life in the organization, conflict may ensure. If a person's preference is for an internal locus of control but the organization is very hierarchical and rigid, the resulting struggle is likely to manifest itself as conflict with co-workers and colleagues.

Interest-based conflict is very common. When departments clash, project team effectiveness suffers. Often the clash is due to perceived differences in status or importance between the divisions. Studies show that teams are only effective when all the team members understand and appreciate the interdependencies within the group.

Informational conflict highlights the importance of solid communication channels. For example, an organization changes its budgetary planning process, including all the rules that affect the budget, without communicating the changes to employees. The result is chaos and hard feelings. Or a new policy comes down that says you must fill out a standard form to make your budgetary requirements known for the upcoming fiscal year. If the sheet is not filled out, you won't get the money. You fill out the sheet and see the line item show up in your budget. Then you discover that other managers have access to what you thought were your resources, because money is tight this year and another policy (which was never officially released) says resources will be allocated to the most critical requirements. You didn't know about this policy, so you're not prepared to fight for your money.

Cultural conflict is all around us. As the workplace becomes more and more culturally diverse, these kinds of conflict are occurring with increasing frequency. When we work to resolve conflict, we must have the discipline to seek out the root cause and not presume that we know why people behave as they do.

Interpersonal conflict can occur between manager and employee or between employee and employee. When we see conflict at work, it often looks like it's interpersonal, because it most often plays out between two people. But appearances can be misleading. It's important to spend time discerning and treating the *real* cause of any conflict in order to cultivate a work environment in which the group dynamic is focused on unified intentions and shared goals.

Gender-related conflict can be more subtle in group dynamics. As gender roles have become less defined, women and men continue to struggle with blending and merging their tendencies and preferences, especially at work. And as more organizations adopt team-based approaches, people must learn to effectively manage multiple professional relationships. Poor relations between men and women are a significant source of performance problems, yet there are few attempts to comprehend and resolve this type of interpersonal tension. Understanding the characteristic differences between men and women can help us adapt to and complement each other's gifts and natural talents. Successful executives know they benefit most from a healthy balance of the strengths of both men and women in the workplace.

Our culture teaches us from a very young age that conflict is bad. It means that people are angry, unhappy and upset. While it's true that some degree of emotion is the basis of every conflict, we have to reorient our thinking and see that conflict can be a very good thing and a critical factor in our quest for continuous improvement and resolving issues. Psychologists cite a phenomenon called "pseudo-community" to describe groups that co-exist at a superficial level. By contrast, one of the ingredients of effective teams is a high degree of trust.

Trust is very difficult to foster and maintain when the team is in pseudo-community, because no one wants to rock the boat. In such cases, conflict is the means by which relationships can move forward and trust can be built. Our long-standing aversion to conflict is due to our tendency to equate it with angry outbursts, emotion and giving up what we want. But if we change our attitude about conflict, we can get different results.

There are proven ways to get at the heart of conflict. One is to remember that people seldom intend to be in conflict and most welcome the chance to move out of conflict. As leaders, we might help by looking beyond the source of a conflict. There are two factors at the heart of every conflict: (1) a position and (2) underlying interests. Effective conflict management distinguishes between the somewhat emotional positions people take based on what they want or expect in a situation and the underlying interests that may not be apparent to anyone in the dynamic.

Substantive interests are about the topic at hand; for example, a performance appraisal or the price of a car. There are always substantive interests in any conflict. *Process-based interests* are directly related to conflict modes and preferences. When someone with a hard-line, competitive style comes up against someone with a cooperative style, there's going to be conflict. These are the biggest conflict challenges, because they sometimes overshadow the substantive issues. *Relationship-based interests* focus on the value each party places on the relationship. This is a particularly important aspect in large projects with cross-functional teams and ongoing operations. Relationship-based interests influence trust, respect, motivation, group unity and enthusiasm.

One way to reduce the intensity of a conflict quickly is to make a distinction between feedback and criticism. Emotion can lead us to judge others or to perceive input as criticism. If it's truly your intention to offer feedback rather than criticism, you'll do whatever it takes to make that happen. It may be as simple as using "I" statements, explaining how something makes you feel, rather than accusatory "you" statements. No two situations are alike, so expressing feedback in a way that is not critical is always a matter of judgment.

Another way to channel the energies of conflict toward a successful outcome is to define your desired outcome in one of two fundamentally different ways: settlement or resolution. When conflict management focuses on changing behaviors only, we can say we've reached a settlement. A competing style is an example of this approach. Emotion really doesn't play a part in influencing the outcome. But because conflict usually includes underlying issues, a settlement may not be enough, because the attitudes have not been addressed. Resolution requires us to deal with a variety of emotions, such as anger. There are many techniques to help defuse anger, but none of them can work until the emotion is acknowledged as a problem.

In the case of workplace conflict, an intervention is anything a facilitator says or does to alter the behavior of an individual or a group. Sometimes the decision to intervene is a judgment call if the problem is relatively minor. An intervention is usually not needed unless a specific behavior or problem becomes a pattern. Intervening is an obligation when the group's progress is delayed or stalled, or one group member makes a personal attack on another.

There are three types of interventions. The first is to change an established behavior pattern by an individual or a group. The second is to help two or more persons reach a consensus when they're having difficulty doing so. The third is used as a last resort. If the first two interventions have failed to produce any improvement, an intervention to gain managerial support is needed.

Negotiation

Conflict resolution and negotiation skills go hand in hand. The same insights and approaches that can help resolve conflict can also be useful in negotiating, because often what is being negotiated is a resolution to a conflict.

The tools for managing a group dynamic involving negotiations include some basic ones. First, do your homework. Adequate planning is key to success. Planning is more than running through the script of how you think the negotiation will play out. It includes knowing what's important to you. Think of negotiation planning along the same lines as conflict resolution. Ask yourself what's more important to you: the relationship or the outcome. The answer will determine what approach you will take.

Define and prioritize the interests and issues that are important to all the parties. Understand any links or conflicts among them. Know your own limits and alternatives. Set targets and openings;

visualize the approach that makes you confident about succeeding. Assess and analyze the other party. Finalize your strategy, and always have a Plan B. Don't forget the logistics. Sometimes we focus so much on the substance that we forget the process. Factors such as room location, a formal agenda and a record-keeper might seem like trivial details, but if they're overlooked, the outcome may not be the one you want. And this is important: Be ready to use your creativity to reframe rather than reject a counterproposal. This one factor could change the course of a negotiation.

Agreements

Our cumulative record of agreements forms the essence of how people view us. How we approach and honor commitments is a defining dimension of our life. Over time, our ability to make and manage agreements will determine the strength of our relationships. A leader's personal integrity is very much a part of the range and type of agreements that can be made, reaffirmed and expanded over time.

Relationship management includes how we approach agreements. Ultimately, our performance around our agreements forms the basis of trust others have in us. Our skill in making and managing agreements is critical to strong and lasting relationships, especially relationships that involve people with diverse backgrounds and experiences.

When an agreement breaks down, the first thing to do it to acknowledge the breakdown. Many people don't take this important step; instead, they offer a flood of excuses. Without acknowledgement, conversation about the breakdown can come to a standstill and jeopardize the relationship. Without acknowledgement, natural tendencies may become more pronounced. One thing can lead to another, and tension builds.

It's important that each party go back to the original agreement and seek clarification about such things as the nature of the agreement; what each party heard; and the definition of performance. After the parties have acknowledged the breakdown, they must forge a new understanding regarding future expectations. The new agreement is based on lessons learned from the breakdown. In this way, we can grow from failed agreements and learn how to better manage future commitments.

Adapting

Adapting to differences among people in group dynamics boils down to one thing: treating people with respect. Respect is the cornerstone of the best relationships. Approaching all relationships with a sense of personal integrity and an evolving mastery of one's self means we will treat others with respect and foster strong and long-lasting relationships.

This is the higher meaning of "Do unto others." Treating people with respect sometimes means treating them as we would like to be treated. More often, it means treating them as *they* would like to be treated. There are certainly times when an accommodation that the other person would like is too much of a stretch for us. Ideally, there's a midpoint where neither person feels they've had to "give up" something, where both people feel respected, and no one feels as if they've had to sell their soul. The only way to know what being treated with respect means to another person is to ask, listen and consciously refine our behavior.

The only way to sustain strong relationships that foster transformation is to enter into them ready to communicate our own process of personal transformation and to support the process in others. Relationships are about more than sharing things or tasks; they're about sharing success and growth. They're about adapting to each other and, together, to new challenges.

Integrating Dynamics

Beyond conflict is an ability to use all the skills involved in managing group dynamics to manage organizational crisis, which also relies on networks and relationships for success. Paulette Maehara is president and CEO of the Association of Fundraising Professionals, which represents more than 27,000 members in 180 chapters throughout the United States, Canada, Mexico and China, working to advance philanthropy through advocacy, research, education and certification programs.

Paulette related a story to me about how inclusiveness was crucial in a period of organizational crisis. She was the acting CEO of a Red Cross chapter during a period when the Red Cross as a whole was going through a very difficult controversy. She said, "The center here in D.C. was discovered to have a multitude of problems concerning the safety of the blood supply. As a result, there was concern that tainted blood had gotten into the system." That hadn't actually happened; nevertheless, it became a crisis. As a result of a number of similar incidents throughout the system in the early 1990s, the Red Cross decided to consolidate some of its blood operations. One of those operations was in Washington, where Paulette worked. Her job, working in cooperation with the Red Cross National Blood Program staff, was to close the operation down but, in the meantime, to continue to collect blood. That meant that people who knew in January that they would not have jobs in July were still expected to collect blood and meet targets.

Paulette recalled, "I can't remember how many hospitals we had depending on the blood donated from the American Red Cross, but it was a considerable number. I was faced with the crisis of my life at this point.... This was all quite new to me, and my boss resigned abruptly." Paulette found herself with no real experience and very real responsibility weighing on her. Meanwhile, she was trying to negotiate with two very powerful unions over the change in the structure.

She said, "I had one of those moments: 'Oh, my god! What am I going to do? How am I going to do it? How am I going to continue to collect the blood that's needed, keep people on staff to do that, and be successful in the end without cracking this operation?' I felt like I was about to zoom out of control. So I decided the best path was information. Keep people informed. Include people in the dialogue every step of the way. If I didn't know the answer, I told people I didn't know the answer."

The union appreciated the directness, as did the staff and other operations relying on Paulette. She said, "I met with people frequently. I met with the nurses. I met with the mobile unit assistants. I met with operations collections staff and the volunteer chapter staff. I met with the unions. I met with everybody who wanted to meet with me! In the circumstances, the best you can do is communicate. Well, the end result was, over that seven-month period I think we lost only one person out of 350 to 400 people devoted to this particular operation. It was amazing. We didn't lose any blood collections. We maintained our goals. Everyone was either matriculated into the new group or they went on to other positions, but they didn't leave the employment of the Red Cross during this seven-month period."

Precious human resources had been preserved for the organization's future. Paulette's willingness to communicate openly preserved a huge network of relationships, fostered alliances, and provided as much inclusion as possible—enough so that people trusted management and stayed.

Measuring Results

One of the least understood aspects of relationships at work is that they exist to achieve what is intended. They often achieve even more, but requirements exist to measure results. We must be willing and able to test what is achieved against what was expected. Relationships in a culture of transformation support the performance of individuals and of the organization itself. Benchmarks and means for measuring achievement in impartial ways are cornerstones for any organization in transformation; at TSI, we design tools to measure results on a regular basis.

Winston Churchill had an effective and instantaneous method of measuring results. Throughout his long and transformative career, Churchill had many vocal detractors. Under similar circumstances, many leaders would react defensively; most would certainly not add to the chorus of criticism. Yet, a very important part of Churchill's success was his disciplined self-criticism. Every day, he critiqued his work. "Every night," he remarked to one of his aides, "I try myself by court martial to see if I have done anything effective during the day. I don't mean just pawing the ground, anyone can go through the motions, but something really effective."[29] Churchill meant business, and he was not deterred in his focus on consciously evolving by any private wish to refute his opponents or ignore his shortcomings.

As if his nightly "court martial" wasn't enough, Churchill sought feedback and advice from colleagues and subordinates. He welcomed criticism from any quarter. A research assistant who worked with him in the 1930s on *A History of the English-Speaking Peoples* attested to Churchill's commitment to consider all feedback as valuable. He said Churchill "always took criticism very, very seriously. One could say exactly what one liked in the way of criticism. He wanted the full critical value from subordinates."[30] Before he became prime minister in 1940, Churchill served again, briefly, as first lord of the admiralty. On his first day, in 1939, he sent a clear message to the senior staff by concluding a memo with this wish: "The First Lord submits these notes to his naval colleagues for consideration, *for criticism and correction,* and hopes to receive proposals for action in the sense desired."[31]

For a leader, feedback is a tool; like any tool, it must be used with skill or it can cause more harm than good. As Bob Sledd's experience as CEO of Performance Food Group showed, a leader can benefit by valuing his own mistakes as lessons. Bob did not hide his mistakes, and he set an example for those around him to learn from their mistakes, too. Without his willingness to criticize himself, he could not have led Performance Food Group to a market leader position. For Bob—and for any leader who seeks to transform an organization—criticism is a tool that does not damage but frees the best of ourselves to come forward and participate.

The most valuable source of feedback is the relationships we have with other people, whether it's a one-to-one peer relationship, a team, or a diverse network among colleagues and staff members. Regardless of the nature of the relationship, building bonds at work can make all links in the organizational chain stronger. Relationships are the path to continuously relaying everything from information and a sense of purpose to energy and spirited morale.

People in relationships influence each other's thoughts, feelings and behaviors. Our workplaces are complex networks of relationships, and the work we do—whether functional, transformational or crisis driven—is influenced by our connections to co-workers. Skillful relationship management is critical to our professional effectiveness; it enables us to manage the pathways of energy, inspiration, expertise and possibility throughout our networks.

If we have the ability to manage relationships, we are better equipped to be valuable team members ourselves. All people want to feel cared about and respected by others. Most people respond with the best of themselves if they believe they're contributing to an effort that is working well; that they're valued and succeeding. Here is where the leader's personal integrity comes into play, setting the tone for success, which includes taking risks and making mistakes on the way. But while the leader might embody these and other values, it's the relationships among contributors that reinforce and support them—and embed them in the culture of an organization in transformation.

One very easy way to monitor and manage the impact of our behavior in relationships is to ask for feedback. Unfortunately, people often wait for work relationships to become strained or damaged before they seek feedback. Interestingly enough, the feedback already exists in the giver's mind—all the receiver has to do is ask for it. People notice and remember details about other people's performance. They notice behaviors and actions that create successes and failures. People like to give feedback but are sometimes fearful of creating hurt feelings by offering it. When we request feedback (as opposed to waiting for someone to offer it), we're demonstrating our receptivity. Feedback is a precious gift—it's okay to ask for it.

Dr. Renato DiPentima, former president and CEO of SRA International, shared his reflections on how relationships are like networks, carrying the energy, expertise and information that can uplift entire groups to new levels of success. Renny said, "When I think about organizations, I've been taught to think about them in two graphic representations. One is the performance of the individual, and the other is the performance of the company. Even while the performance of the individual gets better and better, sometimes it has very little impact on the company. Then there are companies where there is a direct relationship between the individual and the company's performance. These days, I usually find in a bureaucracy—not only the government but any big bureaucracy—the individual can get lost in the process."

He went on, "The best police officer of the Baltimore or Washington police force, who has had great training and knows everything there is to know, will have very little positive effect on the overall performance of the police department. He could, however, have an enormous negative litigious effect if he used his gun and shot someone. So the reason bureaucracies work as they do—by moving people up very slowly over great periods of time—is to actually protect against this potential negative performance. Now look at a different model, a model where the direct performance of the person affects the performance of the team. For example, if Jim Palmer did great, the Baltimore Orioles did great. If John Elway performs well, the Denver Broncos do well. Very rarely in a company can one person have this effect. But it happens. There is Lee Iacocca, who, with the force of his personality, can cause the whole company to do well. On the other side, there was Ken Lay."

As Renny considers how to create a culture where individuals can have an impact, he believes "generally that's around building teams that are focused on an outcome and have excellent leaders, not only managers, but excellent leaders. And if you look at that, which I have many times, you can see a whole series of successes where that model applies—where everybody on the team feels that their performance can have direct impact on overall performance and outcome. They're not a cog in the wheel. They're not going to get lost. Everything they're doing contributes directly to the success of the team. Very rarely are you going to find one individual who can point to a really, truly excellent outcome and can say 'I did it all.'"

Renny gave me an example based on a prior experience when the government was faced with a large amount of down-sizing. Social Security was being downsized, and Renny was an Associate Commissioner at the time. He was working with a Frederick Taylor-like production line process in which information was gathered by one person and passed on to others for processing. If the information came back a day or two later indicating something was wrong with the information input, the whole process would start again. Someone would have to find the folder and restart the process. Data was all paper and only moved as fast as paper. No one could imagine anything less cumbersome.

After nine months of little progress on streamlining the process, Renny was asked to step in and manage it. "We did it by building a real team environment around important people throughout the organization," Renny recalled. "We empowered them to make the decisions that affected them. We challenged the Systems Team by saying 'Let's build a Social Security office in this building to look like one of our 2,000 offices. When you see it, you will think you are in a Social Security office. If we are as smart as we think we are, let's show how we can modernize that office. Let's show how we can get off paper and into a fully online interactive environment.'"

"At that time, it could take weeks to get information from our databases because everything was on paper. The team drew up a concept of what a modern environment would look like. I said, "Let's do it. Here are the rules—I'll provide the resources, but the systems folks have to live outside the office, and we'll bring in real SSA employees from offices around the company to staff the office. They will come in six months at a time, and they will run this office as though it is a real Social Security office. We will use existing applications and show how we can build and transition to a modern, online interactive process and system.'" And they did it in less than twelve months. Their work was even the first government agency featured by Tom Peters in his film, *Thriving on Chaos*.

"We then set up some pilot offices and started to take electronic applications. I still remember the first electronic application. We chose the employee who ran the model office to go to York, Pennsylvania, and take the first official application. After that office was successfully running under the new process, we built nineteen more, including an office in Washington, DC. We invited Congressmen and staff to visit and see it. When they said, 'I want one of these in my district,' we would ask them to support the $479.1 million budget we had submitted to the Hill. And, we would say, 'When the budget is approved, there will be one of these in your district.' Because of what they actually saw, our budgets were approved. It was an environment where everyone came out a winner, and everyone was very proud to have been associated with the project. Our employees received lots of awards and recognition, and there was a great deal of camaraderie by people thinking they had made the journey together."

In leading his team to transform an entire government agency, I'm struck by how Renny integrated all the functions involved in the administrative system to achieve a new, streamlined approach more in keeping with cutting-edge technology. Leadership often involves integrating disparate parts. We integrate diverse people with diverse points of view, especially in managing conflict and other high-energy interpersonal dynamics. Even more fundamentally, we embark on a process of personal transformation that leads us to challenge and integrate a great range of abilities and experiences in ourselves. Personal mastery, at the heart of it, is a process of transformation and integration.

CHAPTER NINE

Full-Circle Integrity

Growing Networks of Exchange and Creative Power

Any book about leadership must conclude by reflecting on the role of integrity in what we seek to achieve. That applies even to leadership books that open, as this one does, with a discussion of integrity.

For transformation to occur at all, personal mastery relies on personal integrity, and that is why integrity is crucial for a leader in motion. Effective personal mastery transforms the leader, who in turn transforms the interpersonal dynamics in which he operates by cultivating a culture of transformation. The leader has many roles—the more we, as leaders, personally master ourselves, the more we are able to positively influence all the different types of bonds in our organization. Teams, networks, meetings, friendships—all can be recast for success by a leader's clarity, commitment and energy.

The leader's role is to recognize and promote respect among diverse participants and to cultivate unified intention in working groups. These dynamic relationships sometimes come into conflict within themselves and with other groups, but they can also work in harmony. By encouraging harmony and striking a balance among many different parts of a group, the leader integrates the many to engage one vision with one heart. The leader is an integrator.

So, while this book opens by talking about the critical need for leaders with integrity, it closes by taking a look at how leaders also foster organizational integrity. Leaders create a unity of purpose and a harmony among parts. This role is crucial—in the new world reality, a variety of tasks, talents and personalities are at work. Here, leadership integrates. We manage the power of others in order to welcome dynamic creativity and foster balance within the group. We model respect for diversity of opinion and style, and encourage openness among participants in the group. This ensures that cooperation replaces competition. We shepherd all the best talent toward a shared goal.

This is how leaders transform the chaos of creativity into unity. They create balance within creative diversity. In unity, the group becomes productive and enjoys shared achievement. The organization operates with unrivaled capacity and competes readily in the demanding new world reality.

All this can happen only because leaders are in motion and stay in motion, with the intention to make a positive difference.

Scott Sink, executive in residence at the College of Engineering at Ohio State University, has been a great mentor throughout my career. Scott wrote to me that "Integrity .. has to do with the extent to which thought, word, deed are aligned, are consistent.... It's internal and external consistency." He was getting at the idea of organizational integrity and the leader's central role in securing it. Or, as Kalpesh Desai, CEO of Agile Financial Technologies (based in Dubai), says, "Leading with integrity is a quality where a leader ensures that his or her environment is maintained in an unbroken state."

C. Venugopal, managing director and CEO of Krysalis Consultancy Services Pvt., Ltd. (India), expressed it best when he said, "Integrity, the word itself, holds the answer to your interesting question. It shares a common root with several other interesting words: *integral*, meaning 'essential' or 'containing all parts that are necessary,' and *integrate*, meaning 'combining meaningfully' or 'making someone fully a member of a community.' Don't you see your answer emerging? What is leadership? It is creating the ambience that allows a disparate group to combine meaningfully to perform a task at hand. Leadership therefore, integrates. So, to your question, can leadership exist without Integrity? Obviously not."

So, we come full circle to the first quality of leadership, whether it's formal or informal, and that is integrity. Integrity is not just the starting point for the kind of sustainable transformation needed in today's world environment. A leader with integrity can, by example, relay the commitment to continuous transformation, in which all the disparate parts necessary to function are present in balance and harmony.

The race to win organizational health, wealth and creative power begins with personal mastery, and the journey toward personal mastery begins with a commitment to integrity. Leaders with integrity are integrators of diverse people, talents and capabilities, creating meaningful combinations in projects, meetings, teams and daily decisions. Constantly integrating new ideas, opportunities and possibilities into the mix, leaders lead best when they are leaders in motion.

Leadership is integrity in motion.

Endnotes

1. For Hopper's biography, see Naval Historical Center, "Biographies in Naval History: Rear Admiral Grace Murray Hopper, USN," www.history.nay.mil/bios/hopper_grace.htm, accessed August 28, 2008. For an obituary, see Mitch Betts, "Grace Hopper, Mother of COBOL, Dies," *Computerworld*, January 6, 1992.
2. Michael Dell with Catherine Fredman, *Direct from Dell: Strategies That Revolutionized an Industry* (New York: HarperBusiness, 1999), 12–15.
3. For more information about Alfred Mann, see Associated Press, "USC Gets $100 Million Donation," February 5, 1998; David Whelan, "$100 Million, Anyone?" *Forbes*, October 6, 2006; Guy Griml, "Technion Receives $100 Million Donation," Haaretz, October 15, 2006; Goldie Bluemnstyk "Purdue to House $100 Million Biomedical Institute Paid for by Mann Foundation," *Chronicle of Higher Education*, March 30, 2007.
4. Elizabeth Smith Brownstein, *Lincoln's Other White House: The Untold Story of the Man and His Presidency* (Hoboken, NJ: Wiley, 2005), 113–121.
5. Winston S. Churchill, *Painting as a Pastime* (Delray Beach, FL: Levenger, 2002).
6. Ben Stein, *How Successful People Win: Using "Bunkhouse Logic" To Get What You Want Out of Life* (Carlsbad, CA: Hay House, 2005).

7. "Vision" entry in Online Etymology dictionary, www.etymon-line.com.index.php?search=vision&searchmode=none, accessed September 9, 2008.

8. Randolph S. Churchill, *Winston S. Churchill, Volume II: Young Statesman, 1901–1914* (Boston: Houghton Mifflin, 1967), 558.

9. Martin Gilbert, *Winston S. Churchill, Volume IV: The Stricken World, 1916–1922* (Boston: Houghton Mifflin, 1975), 190.

10. Winston S. Churchill, *The Second World War. Volume 4, The Hinge of Fate* (Boston: Houghton Mifflin, 1950), 66.

11. Steven F. Hayward, *Churchill on Leadership: Executive Success in the Face of Adversity* (Rocklin, CA: ICS Press/Prima, 1997), 128.

12. Martin S. Gilbert, *Winston S. Churchill, Volume IV: The Stricken World, 1916–1922* (Boston: Houghton Mifflin, 1975), 526.

13. Sir John Wheeler-Bennett (ed.), *Action This Day: Working With Churchill* (New York: St. Martin's, 1969), 235.

14. Martin S. Gilbert, *The Churchill War Papers, Volume 1: At the Admiralty, September 1939–May 1940* (New York: Norton, 1993), 91.

15. Martin S. Gilbert, *Winston S. Churchill, Volume V: The Prophet of Truth, 1922–1939* (Boston: Houghton Mifflin, 1977), 617.

16. Martin S. Gilbert, *Winston S. Churchill, Volume VI: Finest Hour, 1939–1941* (Boston: Houghton Mifflin, 1983), 156.

17. Winston S. Churchill, *The Second World War, Volume 1: The Gathering Storm* (Boston: Houghton Mifflin, 1948), 695.

18. Paul Addison, *Churchill on the Home Front, 1900–1955* (Boston: Pimlico, 1993), 110.

19. Winston S. Churchill (grandson, ed.), *Never Give In! The Best of Winston Churchill's Speeches* (New York: Hyperion, 1993), 266–274.

20. Stephen Mansfield, *Never Give In: The Enduring Character of Winston Churchill* (Nashville, TN: Cumberland House, 1996), 148–149.

21. American Institute of Stress, "Stress Reduction," stress.org/stress_reduction.htm, accessed December 5, 2008.

22. John T. Molloy, *Molloy's Live for Success* (New York: Perigord Press/Morrow, 1981), 37.

23. Sam Walton with John Huey, *Made in America: My Story* (New York: Doubleday, 1992), 247.

24. Numerous polls report that poor communication is the #1 office problem, including "Employees Most Frustrated by Lack of Communication in the Workplace, Opinion Research Corporation Finds," *Business Wire,* November 7, 2007.

25. David Herbert Donald, *Lincoln* (New York: Simon and Schuster, 1995), 62–64.

26. Philip Van Doren Stern (ed.), *The Life and Writings of Abraham Lincoln* (New York: Modern Library, 1940), 263.

27. Carol Wilson and L. Richard Hoffman, "Managers as Negotiators: A Test of Power Versus Gender as Predictors of Feelings, Behavior, and Outcomes," *Leadership Quarterly,* Winter 1996.

28. Steve Kaufer and Jurg W. Mattman, "The Cost of Workplace Violence to American Business," www.workviolence.com/articles/cost_of_workpl;ace_violence.htm, accessed September 8, 1998.

29. Gilbert, *The Finest Hour,* 759.

30. Gilbert, *The Prophet of Truth,* 501.

31. Churchill, *The Gathering Storm,* 427–428.

Bibliography

Addison, Paul. *Churchill on the Home Front, 1900–1955.* London: Pimlico, 1993.

Allen, David. *Getting Things Done: The Art of Stress-Free Productivity.* New York: Viking, 2001.

Axelrod, Alan, and Jim Holtje. *201 Ways to Deal With Difficult People.* New York: McGraw-Hill, 1990.

Baker, William F. *Leading with Kindness: How Good People Consistently Get Superior Results.* New York, AMACOM, 2008.

Barnett, Rosalind C, Lois Biener, and Grace K. Baruch (eds.). *Gender and Stress.* New York: Free Press, 1987.

Bens, Ingrid. *Facilitating With Ease: A Step-By-Step Guidebook With Customizable Worksheets on CD-ROM.* San Francisco: Jossey-Bass, 2000.

Bowman-Kestner, Prudence, and Larry Ray. *The Conflict Resolution Training Program.* San Francisco: Jossey-Bass, 1992.

Brownstein, Elizabeth Smith. *Lincoln's Other White House: The Untold Story of the Man and His Presidency.* Hoboken, NJ: Wiley, 2005.

Butler, Katherine. *StressBusters: Tips to Feel Healthy, Alive, and Energized.* Minneapolis: Chronimed Publishers, 1998.

Carlson, Richard. *Don't Sweat The Small Stuff at Work: Simple Ways to Minimize Stress and Conflict While Bringing Out the Best in Yourself and Others.* New York: Hyperion, 1998.

Carnegie, Dale. *How to Stop Worrying and Start Living.* New York: Simon and Schuster, 1948.

Caroselli, Marlene. *The Big Book of Meeting Games: 75 Quick, Fun Activities For Leading Creative, Energetic, Productive Meetings.* New York: McGraw-Hill, 2002.

Churchill, Randolph. *Winston S. Churchill. Volume 2: Young Statesman.* Boston: Houghton Mifflin, 1967.

Churchill, Winston S. *Painting as a Pastime.* Delray Beach, Florida: Levenger, 2002.

Churchill, Winston S. *The Second World War, Volume 1: The Gathering Storm.* Boston: Houghton Mifflin, 1948.

Churchill, Winston S. *The Second World War, Volume 4: The Hinge of Fate.* Boston: Houghton Mifflin, 1950.

Churchill, Winston S. *The Wit and Wisdom of Winston Churchill: A Treasury of More Than 1,000 Quotations and Anecdotes.* Edited by James C. Humes. New York: HarperCollins, 1994.

Cloke, Kenneth, and Joan Goldsmith. *Resolving Conflicts at Work: A Complete Guide for Everyone on the Job.* San Francisco: Jossey-Bass, 2000.

Cockerell, Lee. *Creating Magic: 10 Common Sense Leadership Strategies from a Life at Disney.* New York: Doubleday, 2008.

Cohen, Eliot A. *Supreme Command: Soldiers, Statesmen, and Leadership in Wartime.* New York: Free Press, 2002.

Collins, Jim. *Good to Great: Why Some Companies Make the Leap—and Others Don't.* New York: HarperBusiness, 2001.

Cook, Marshall. *Streetwise Time Management: Get More Done With Less Stress By Efficiently Managing Your Time.* Holbrook, MA: Adams Media, 1999.

Covey, Stephen, A. Roger Merrill, and Rebecca R. Merrill. *First Things First: To Live, To Love, To Learn, To Leave a Legacy.* New York: Simon and Schuster, 1998.

Craven, Robin, and Lynn Johnston Gulabowski, with D'Etta Wallach. *Complete Idiot's Guide to Meeting and Event Planning.* Second edition. New York: Alpha Books, 2000.

Crowe, Sandra A. *Since Strangling Isn't an Option: Dealing With Difficult People—Common Problems and Uncommon Solutions.* New York: Perigee, 1999.

Csikszentmihalyi, Mihaly. *Flow: The Psychology of Deep Experience.* New York: Harper and Row, 1990.

Dana, Daniel. *Conflict Resolution: Mediation Tools for Everyday Worklife.* New York: McGraw-Hill, 2001.

Davis. Martha, Elizabeth Robbins Eshelman, and Matthew McKay. *The Relaxation and Stress Reduction Workbook.* Sixth edition. Oakland, CA: New Harbinger Publications, 2008.

Dell, Michael, with Catherine Fredman. *Direct From Dell: Strategies That Revolutionized an Industry.* New York: HarperBusiness, 1999.

Donald, David Herbert. *Lincoln.* New York: Simon and Schuster, 1995.

Doyle, Michael, and David Straus. *How to Make Meetings Work.* New York: Berkley, 1993.

Eberhardt, Louise Yolton. *Bridging the Gender Gap.* Duluth, MN: Whole Person Associates, 1995.

Emmett, Rita. *The Procrastinator's Handbook: Mastering the Art of Doing It Now.* New York: Walker, 2000.

Fisher, Roger, and William Ury. *Getting to Yes: Negotiating Agreements and Not Giving In.* New York: Penguin, 1991.

Fox, Sue. *Business Etiquette for Dummies.* Second edition. Indianapolis: Wiley, 2008.

Fritz, Robert. *The Path of Least Resistance: Learning to Become the Creative Person in Your Own Life.* Second edition. New York: FawcettColumbine, 1999.

Gilbert, Martin. *The Churchill War Papers, Volume 1: At the Admiralty, September 1939–May 1940.* New York: Norton, 1993.

Gilbert, Martin. *Winston S. Churchill, Volume 4: The Stricken World, 1916–1922.* Boston: Houghton Mifflin, 1975.

Gilbert, Martin. *Winston S. Churchill, Volume 5: The Prophet of Truth, 1922–1939.* Boston: Houghton Mifflin, 1977.

Gilbert, Martin. *Winston S. Churchill, Volume 6: Finest Hour, 1939–1941.* Boston: Houghton Mifflin, 1983.

Gillespie, Kris, and Brian Gillespie. *When Mama Ain't Happy, Ain't Nobody Happy.* Tulsa: Insight Publishers, 1999.

Glass, Lillian. *He Says, She Says: Closing the Communication Gap Between the Sexes.* New York: Putnam, 1992.

Godin, Seth. *Tribes: We Need You to Lead Us.* New York: Portfolio, 2008.

Gordon, Jon. *The Energy Bus: 10 Rules to Fuel Your Life, Work, and Team with Positive Energy.* New York: John Wiley & Sons. Inc. 2008.

Goleman, Daniel. *Working With Emotional Intelligence.* New York: Bantam, 1998.

Gray, John. *Mars and Venus in the Workplace: A Practical Guide for Improving Communication and Getting Results at Work.* New York: HarperCollins, 2002.

Griessman, B. Eugene. *Time Tactics of Very Successful People.* New York: McGraw-Hill, 1994.

Guttman, Howard M. *When Goliaths Clash: Managing Executive Conflict to Build a More Dynamic Association.* New York: American Management Association, 2003.

Hawkins, Charlie. *First Aid for Meetings.* Wilsonville, OR: Book Partners, 1997.

Hayward, Steven F. *Churchill on Leadership: Executive Success in the Face of Adversity.* Rocklin, CA: ICS Press/Prima, 1997.

Hendricks, Gay, and Kate Ludeman. *The Corporate Mystic: A Guidebook for Visionaries With Their Feet on the Ground.* New York: Bantam, 1996.

Hunter, Dale, Anne Bailey, and Bill Taylor. *The Art of Facilitation: How to Create Group Synergy.* Tucson: Fisher Books, 1995.

Hunter, Dale, Anne Bailey, and Bill Taylor. *Zen of Groups: A Handbook for People Meeting With a Purpose.* Tucson: Fisher Books, 1995.

Jenks, James M., and John M. Kelly. *Don't Do: Delegate!* New York: Franklin Watts, 1985.

Kearney, Katherine, and Thomas I. White. *Men and Women at Work.* Hawthorne, NJ: Career Press, 1994.

Kiyosaki, Robert, with Sharon Lechter. *Rich Dad, Poor Dad: What the Rich Teach Their Kids about Money—That the Poor and Middle-Class Do Not!* New York: Warner Books, 2000.

Kunhardt, Philip B., Jr., Philip B. Kunhardt III, and Peter W. Kunhardt. *Lincoln: An Illustrated Biography.* New York: Knopf, 1992.

LaRoche, Loretta. *Life Is Not a Stress Rehearsal: Bringing Yesterday's Sane Wisdom Into Today's Insane World.* New York: Broadway Books, 2001.

Lewicki, Roy, et al., *Negotiation.* Burr Ridge, IL: Irwin, 1994.

Mackenzie, Alex. *The Time Trap.* New York: MJF Books, 2002.

Meyer, Jeffrey J. *Time Management for Dummies.* Second edition. Foster City, CA: IDG Books Worldwide, 1999.

Micale, Frances A. *Not Another Meeting! A Practical Guide for Facilitating Effective Meetings.* Second edition. Central Point, OR: Oasis Press, 2002.

Molloy, John T. *Molloy's Live for Success.* New York: Perigord/Morrow, 1981.

Morgenstern, Julie. *Time Management from the Inside Out: The Foolproof System for Taking Care of Your Schedule—And Your Life.* Second edition. New York: Henry Holt, 2004.

Mosvick, Roger B., and Robert B. Nelson. *We've Got to Start Meeting Like This: A Guide for Successful Meeting Management.* Indianapolis: Park Avenue, 1996.

Nichols, Barbara (ed.). *Professional Meeting Management.* Second edition. Birmingham, AL: Professional Convention Management Association, 1989.

Pachter, Barbara, with Susan Magee. *When the Little Things Count—And They Always Count: 601 Essential Things That Everyone in Business Needs to Know.* New York: Marlowe, 2001.

Pearson, Carol. *The Hero Within: Six Archetypes We Live By.* Second edition. San Francisco: HarperSanFrancisco, 1998.

Peeke, Pamela. *Fight Fat After Forty.* New York: Viking, 2000.

Phillips, Donald T. *The Founding Fathers on Leadership.* New York: Warner, 1997.

Phillips, Donald T. *Lincoln on Leadership: Executive Strategies for Tough Times.* New York: Warner, 1992.

Pincus, Marilyn. *Everyday Business Etiquette.* Hauppauge, NY: Barron's, 1996.

Post, Peggy, and Peter Post. *Emily Post's Etiquette Advantage in Business: Personal Skills for Professional Success.* Second edition. New York: HarperResource, 2005.

Powell, Gary N. *Gender and Diversity in the Workplace.* Thousand Oaks, CA: Sage, 1999.

Quinn, Robert E. *Deep Change: Discovering the Leader Within.* San Francisco: Jossey-Bass, 1996.

Random House Book of Etiquette. New York: Random House, 1967. (Random House Hostess Library, v. 1)

Random House Treasury of Cooking. New York: Random House, 1967. (Random House Hostess Library, v. 2)

Sabath, Ann Marie. *Business Etiquette in Brief: The Complete Guide for Today's Professional.* Holbrook, MA: Bob Adams, 1993.

Sapolsky, Robert M. *Why Zebras Don't Get Ulcers: An Updated Guide to Stress, Stress-Related Diseases, and Coping.* New York: W. H. Freeman, 1998.

Scott, Gini Graham. *Work With Me! Resolving Everyday Conflict at Work.* Palo Alto, CA: Davies-Black, 2000.

Siebert, Al. *The Survivor Personality: Why Some People Are Stronger, Smarter, and More Skillful At Handling Life's Difficulties and How You Can Be, Too!* New York: Perigee, 1996.

Sink, D. Scott, and William T. Morris, with Cindy S. Johnston. *By What Method? Are You Developing the Knowledge and Skills to Lead Large-Scale Quality?* Norcross, GA: Industrial Engineering and Management Press, 1995.

Smith, Hyrum W. *The 10 Natural Laws of Successful Time and Life Management: Proven Strategies for Increased Productivity and Inner Peace.* New York: Warner Books, 1999.

Stein, Ben. *How Successful People Win: Using "Bunkhouse Logic" To Get What You Want Out of Life.* Carlsbad, CA: Hay House, 2005.

Stern, Philip Van Doren (ed.). *The Life and Writings of Abraham Lincoln.* New York: Modern Library, 1940.

Stockdale, Jim and Sybil. *In Love and War: The Story of a Family's Ordeal and Sacrifice During The Vietnam War Years.* New York: Harper and Row, 1984.

Swiss, Deborah J. *The Male Mind at Work: A Woman's Guide to Working With Men.* Cambridge, MA: Perseus, 2000.

Tannen, Deborah. *You Just Don't Understand: Women and Men in Conversation.* New York: Morrow, 1990.

Thomas, Kenneth. *Introduction to Conflict Management: Improving Performance Using the TMI.* Palo Alto, CA: CPP, 2004.

Tingley, Judith C. *Genderflex: Ending the Workplace War Between the Sexes.* Phoenix: Performance Improvement Press, 1993.

Trione, Debra (ed.). *A Perfect World: Words and Paintings from Over 50 of America's Most Powerful People.* Kansas City: Andrews McMeel, 2002.

Walton, Sam, with John Huey. *Made in America: My Story.* New York: Doubleday, 1992.

Watson, Carol, and Richard Hoffman. "Managers as Negotiators: A Test of Power Versus Gender as Predictors of Feelings, Behavior, and Outcomes." *Leadership Quarterly,* Winter 1996.

Wheeler-Bennett, Sir John. *Action This Day: Working With Churchill.* New York: St. Martin's, 1969.

Wilson, Marta C., Stephen Hacker, and Cynthia J. Johnston. *Work Miracles: Transform Yourself and Your Organization.* Portland, OR: Insight Press, 1999.

Winston, Stephanie. *The Organized Executive: The Classic Program for Productivity: New Ways to Manage Time, Paper, People, and the Digital Office.* Revised edition. New York: Warner, 2001.

Withers, Bill. *The Conflict Management Skills Workshop: A Trainer's Guide.* New York: AMACOM, 2002.

Withers, Bill, and Keami Lewis. *The Conflict and Communication Activity Book: 30 High-Impact Team Exercises for Adult Learners.* New York: AMACOM, 2003.

Wright, Robert J. *Beyond Time Management: Business With Purpose.* Boston: Butterworth-Heinemann, 2001.

Yager, Jan. *Business Protocol: How to Survive and Succeed in Business.* Second edition. Stamford, CT: Hannacroix Creek Books, 2001.

Young, Cathy. *Ceasefire! Why Women and Men Must Join Forces to Achieve True Equality.* New York: Free Press, 1999.

Zeer, Darrin. *Office Yoga: 75 Simple Stretches for Busy People.* San Francisco: Chronicle Books, 2005.

Index

Transformation Systems, Inc.

Founded in 1994 by Marta C. Wilson, Transformation Systems, Inc. (TSI) is a woman-owned small business headquartered in Arlington, VA with bases of operation in Washington, DC, Richmond, VA and Atlanta, GA. Time and time again, TSI has proven to be on target while enthusiastically exceeding customer expectations and building a track record of outcomes including significant cost reductions and exceptional revenue leaps.

Recognized by clients as the source for world-class workplace transformation solutions, TSI helps leaders achieve their audacious goals for a faster, better and smarter organization. Executives seek assistance from TSI's interdisciplinary team of experts whose advanced credentials and experience in engineering, psychology, business and evaluation provide the edge to catalyze positive change and solve complex problems while achieving measurable and sustainable success.

TSI offers consultative services in organizational change facilitation; strategic and implementation planning; professional development training; leadership coaching; and comprehensive results measurement.

Wilson has written, "As the founder of TSI, I serve as a leader among my valued colleagues, all of whom are experts in transformation. We are regularly invited to overhaul performance on individual, group and organizational levels. How do we do this? We do it by keeping leaders in motion."

For more information about TSI, please visit
www.transformationsystems.com.